How to Make Super Pop-ups

By Joan Irvine

Illustrated by Linda Hendry

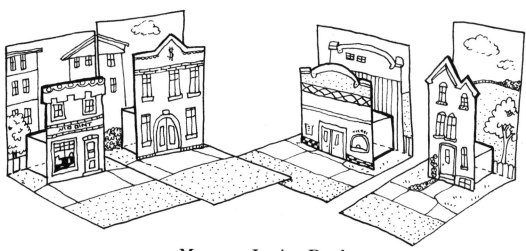

Morrow Junior Books
New York

Text copyright © 1992 by Joan Irvine
Illustrations copyright © 1992 by Linda Hendry
First published in Canada in 1992 by Kids Can Press, 585½ Bloor
Street West, Toronto, Ontario, Canada M6G 1K5.

1 2 3 4 5 6 7 8 9 10

Library of Congress Cataloging-in-Publication Data
Irvine, Joan, 1951–
    How to make super pop-ups / by Joan Irvine;
illustrated by Linda Hendry.   p.   cm.
    Summary: Provides instructions for making a variety
of paper pop-ups, including animals, boats, robots, and
enormous pop-ups for the stage.
    ISBN 0-688-10690-0 (trade).—ISBN 0-688-10691-9 (library).
    1. Paper work—Juvenile literature.   2. Paper toy
making—Juvenile literature.   [1. Paper toy making.
2. Toy making. 3. Handicraft.] I. Hendry, Linda, ill. II. Title.
TT870.I78   1992 745.569—dc20 92-2637 CIP AC

Contents

This book is dedicated to my husband, Steve,
who was incredibly supportive and helpful in
the writing of *How to Make Super Pop-ups*.

Acknowledgements

I would like to thank my family, Elly, Seth and Steve, for their patience and support during the writing of this book. A great thank you goes to my daughter, Elly, who tested many of the ideas in *How to Make Super Pop-ups*. Sarah Bailey, Margaret Loney, Johanna Martin and Laura Burns tested some super pop-ups as well. My sister, Mary Hopkinson, a children's librarian, was very helpful in finding resources.

Thank you to the many children at Keppel-Sarawak School, Owen Sound, Ontario, who tried pop-up techniques in my art classes.

I would like to acknowledge the children in the state of Utah who nominated my book *How to Make Pop-ups* for the 1990 Utah Children's Informational Book Award. The award encouraged me to create new ideas for children who love to make pop-ups!

A great thank you goes to my editor, Liz MacLeod, who helped enormously in improving the manuscript. I also want to thank Michael Solomon for his beautiful and easy-to-follow book design, and Linda Hendry for her wonderful and fun illustrations.

Finally, I would like to acknowledge the support and encouragement from Valerie Hussey and Ricky Englander of Kids Can Press, Canada; and David Reuther of Morrow Junior Books, in the United States.

Introduction

It has been very exciting for me over the past few years to see children enjoying making pop-ups. After receiving requests from children and adults for new pop-up ideas, I began watching children work, collecting new ideas, doing research and now I have written *How to Make Super Pop-ups*.

What are super pop-ups? If you have seen a pop-up book, you will know that it's full of paper figures that pop out toward you or move across the page. Super pop-ups will do those things and more. With this book, you can create a character that juggles, design a pop-up mask and even make Pinocchio's nose grow. You can also create a robot that makes a noise or a pop-up that snaps on a rubber band.

Pop-ups go back a long way in history. Pop-ups using cardboard strips made arms and faces move in early Victorian Valentine cards. In 1860, a British company called Dean and Son published pop-up books known as *Children's Moveable Books*.

You are carrying on a very long tradition by making your own pop-up greeting cards and books. You can also make a centrepiece or a display for a school project. Some pop-ups in this book can even be used for making masks and props for plays and shows.

Making super pop-ups is a great way to recycle material you'd usually throw out. Did you know that you can create pop-ups using envelopes, Popsicle sticks and boxes?

You will be able to use this book without having read *How to Make Pop-ups*. The basic pop-up techniques that you need from that book are repeated at the end of this book.

You can begin with a super pop-up idea from any of the sections. Follow the instructions carefully for cutting and folding. Take your time, be patient and you will have wonderful results.

Materials

To make your super pop-ups, you will need the following materials.

Paper For pop-ups that will last, use heavy paper such as construction paper or light Bristol board. Lighter weight paper can be used for pop-ups that don't get much wear and tear. The instructions will tell you when to use Bristol board or cardboard.

Scissors A sharp pair of scissors with pointed ends are good for cutting paper. Remember to use all cutting equipment with care.

Cutting blade An Olfa touch knife or any other kind of craft knife is useful for making a cut in the middle of a page. Ask an adult to help when you need to use a cutting blade.

Ruler Use a ruler for measurements given in the instructions. A metal ruler will help you make crisp folds and guide your cutting blade.

Glue With light paper, use a glue stick. With heavy paper, use white glue. Always apply glue sparingly and keep glue clear of all moving parts of your pop-up. When you glue two pieces of paper together, a strip of glue on each side is usually enough.

Pencil, markers, crayons, coloured pencils, paints Use an erasable pencil for marking measurements and for designing your drawings. Then go over your pencil drawings with colour.

Brass fasteners These fasteners, which are used for moving circles, are available at stationery or business supply stores. Make sure to use a small size.

String, rubber bands, fabrics, buttons, ribbons, gift wrap, feathers, pictures from magazines These materials and others can be glued to your pop-ups as decorations.

Symbols and Definitions

The following symbols and definitions will be useful to you when you use this book.

- Flap: a small piece of paper that hangs loose
- Tab: a small paper insert that can be glued or pulled
- Slot: an opening that works like a pocket
- Spring: a folded device that makes an object pop up
- Sliding strip: a small piece of paper that helps an object to move
- Mountain fold: an upward fold, shaped like a mountain
- Valley fold: a downward fold, shaped like a valley
- Accordion fold: an up-down-up fold or a down-up-down fold, shaped like a fan

- Fold line – – – – – – – –

- Cut line ——————

- Draw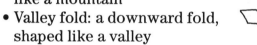

- Colour

- Glue

- Measure

Tips for Folding and Scoring

To make a straight fold on heavy paper, score the paper first. Scoring means making a crease on your paper along the line to be folded. Lay a metal ruler near the line to be folded. Then carefully run the blunt end of a pair of scissors or a ballpoint pen without ink along the fold line. Some people score their paper by running a fingernail across the fold line. When you fold your paper, remember to press firmly.

Tips for Cutting

You will need a sharp pair of scissors for most activities in this book. If you are making a cut in the middle of a page, use a pair of pointed scissors to puncture one of the corners of the cut line before cutting.

A cutting blade, such as an Olfa touch knife, works best to make a cut in the middle of a page. Be careful when using a cutting blade. Adult supervision is recommended.

When you use a cutting blade, a metal ruler will help you guide the knife down the side of the ruler. Always put a board or a thick piece of cardboard under your work, so you don't damage your work space.

Tips for Measuring

All measurements are given in both metric and imperial systems. When you follow the instructions for making a super pop-up, start with one system and stay with it for the whole activity. Measurements differ slightly from system to system.

Part One **Super Cutting**

Would you like to make a flying bird or perhaps an amazing lizard? In Part One, you'll learn special cutting techniques to make these pop-ups and many more.

Super cutting involves cutting, folding and pushing shapes through to the other side of your paper. You'll also discover a new cutting technique called double-cutting. Or try a super pop-up idea that uses three layers of paper instead of two.

In Part One, you'll find many new ways to make creatures and animals. You'll even learn how to make a dragon that will turn into a bird when you flip it upside-down!

Tips

- After you fold your paper in half, always cut on the *folded edge*.
- After you cut your paper, make *firm* folds by going over the fold line with your thumb and index finger.
- It is easier to push your cut shape through to the other side if you hold your paper like a tent.
- If you close your paper and press firmly, the cut shape will remain pushed through to the other side of the paper.
- When you glue the inside and outside papers together, apply glue only to the outer edges of the inside paper.
- Never apply glue near the pop-up shape.
- Making one or more triangle folds on a beak or mouth part will give you some really interesting shapes.
- Design your own pop-ups. Make different cuts on the folded edge of a piece of paper, then fold and push the shapes through to the other side.

Make a Birthday Cake

Try double-cutting to make a really super pop-up.

1 Take two pieces of paper, each 21.5 cm x 28 cm (8½ in. x 11 in.). Fold each paper in half. Put one paper aside.

2 On the folded edge of the other paper, mark two dots, each one 4.5 cm (1¾ in.) from the ends.

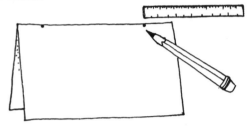

3 Starting at the dots, draw two parallel lines towards the other edge of the paper. Each line should be 2.5 cm (1 in.) long.

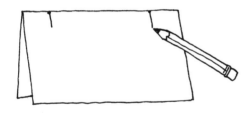

4 Cut the lines, starting from the folded edge.

5 Fold the cut strip forward an back to its original position.

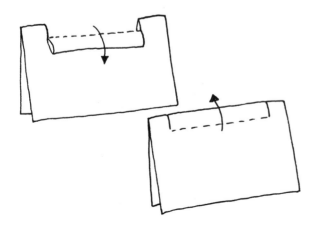

6 Open your paper and hold it like a tent. Push the strip down in the opposite direction of the fold, so that it is pushed through to the other side of your paper. Close the paper and press firmly. Open to see the pop-up strip.

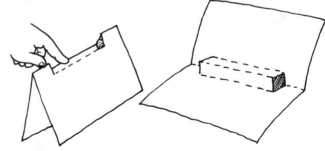

7 Close your paper. On the folded edge of the pop-up strip, mark two dots, each one 2 cm (¾ in.) from the ends.

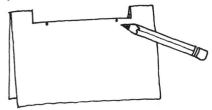

8 Starting at the dots, draw two parallel lines towards the other edge of the paper. Each line should be 2 cm (¾ in.) long. Starting from the folded edge, cut the lines, being careful to cut through only the top fold of your paper. *Do not cut through both folded edges of the pop-up strip.*

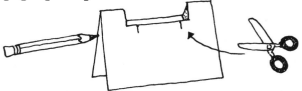

9 Fold the cut strip forward and then fold it back to its original position. Open your paper and push the strip down and through to the other side of your paper. Close the paper and press firmly. Open to see the second pop-up strip.

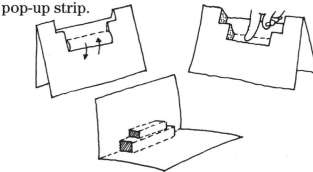

10 Close your paper. On the folded edge of the last pop-up strip, mark two dots, each one 1.6 cm (⅝ in.) from the ends.

11 Starting at the dots, draw two parallel lines towards the other edge of the paper. Each line should be 1.2 cm (½ in.) long.

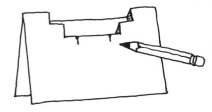

12 Cut the lines, starting from the folded edge. Again, do not cut through both folded edges of the pop-up strip. Fold the strip forward and then fold it back to its original position.

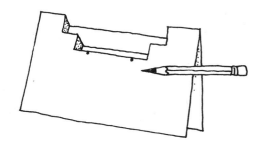

13 Open your paper and push the strip down and through to the other side of your paper. Close the paper and press firmly. Open to see the third pop-up strip.

14 Close your paper. On the folded edge of the last pop-up strip, mark two dots, each one 1.6 cm (⅝ in.) from the ends.

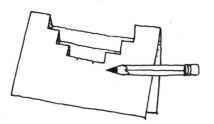

15 Starting at the dots, draw two parallel lines towards the other edge of the paper. Each line should be .6 cm (¼ in.) long.

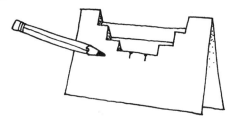

16 Cut the lines as you've done for the other pop-up strips. Fold the strip forward and then fold it back to its original position. Push the strip down and through to the other side of the paper. Close the paper and press firmly. Open to see the fourth pop-up strip.

17 To make the candles for your cake, take a piece of heavy white paper. Draw, colour and cut out the candles.

18 Apply glue to the back of each candle at the bottom. Glue the candles to the front edge of the folded layers of the cake.

19 Now apply glue to the back of your paper. Glue it to the paper you put aside, which now becomes the outside paper. *Do not apply glue in the area of the birthday cake.*

20 Decorate the inside and outside papers.

Other Ideas

Castle

By adding doors, windows and towers with flags, you can make a castle.

Ship

Make a ship by adding portholes, a flag and waves.

Make a Lizard with Amazing Eyes

1 Take two pieces of paper, each 21.5 cm x 28 cm (8½ in. x 11 in.). Fold each paper in half. Put one aside.

2 Place the other paper so that the folded edge is on your left. Mark a dot 8 cm (3⅛ in.) from the bottom of the paper.

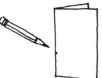

3 From this dot, draw a 6 cm (2¼ in.) diagonal line towards the top right-hand corner of the paper.

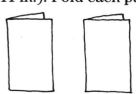

4 Cut the line, starting at the folded edge.

5 Fold the flap back to form a triangle.

6 Fold the flap forward to its original position. Open your paper and hold it like a tent. Put your finger on the tip of the cut shape and push down in the opposite direction of the fold. Then pinch the two folded edges of the shape, so that the shape is pushed through to the other side of the paper. Close the paper and press firmly.

7 When you open your paper and look inside, you will see the pop-up snout of a lizard.

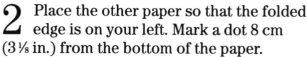

8 To make the amazing eyes, close the paper. On the upper folded edge of the pop-up snout, mark two dots, each one 1 cm (⅜ in.) from the ends.

9 Starting at the dots, draw two parallel lines 1 cm (⅜ in.) long.

10 Cut the two lines, cutting through both folded edges of the pop-up snout.

11 Fold just the top strip back and then fold it forward to its original position.

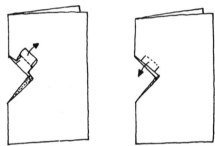

12 Open your paper and push the strip down and through to the other side. Close your paper.

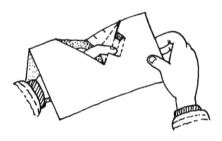

13 Turn to the other side of your paper. Fold the cut strip back and then fold it forward to its original position.

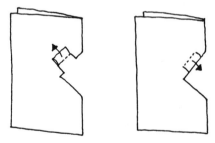

14 Open your paper and push the strip down and through to the other side. You will now have a pair of eyes.

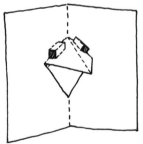

15 Close your paper. On the folded edge of one of the eyes, mark two dots, each one 1 cm (⅜ in.) from the ends.

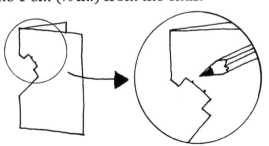

16 Starting at the dots, draw two parallel lines 1 cm (⅜ in.) long.

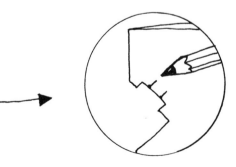

17 Cut the lines, starting from the folded edge. Be careful to cut through only the top fold.

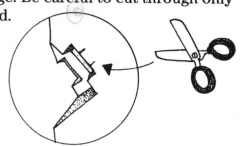

18 Fold the cut strip back and then fold it forward to its original position. Push the strip down and through to the other side.

19 Turn your paper over and repeat steps 15 to 18 on this side of it. Open your paper and you will have two amazing eyes.

20 Glue paper circles to the eyes. Draw and colour a lizard's body around the pop-up face.

21 Apply glue to the back of your paper. Glue it to the paper you put aside, which now becomes the outside paper. *Do not apply glue in the area of the eyes or snout.*

22 Decorate the inside and outside papers.

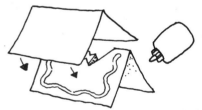

Other Ideas

A Different Snout

Close your paper slightly, then reach inside it and fold the tip of the snout to one side, as shown. Fold the tip back to its original position then push down on it to create an extra fold on the snout. The fold makes the snout point down.

Bird

Follow the directions for "A Different Snout" and draw a bird's head around the pop-up shape.

Make a Catcher's Mask

With this complex cutting technique, you can make pop-ups inside pop-ups.

1 Take two different coloured pieces of heavy paper, each 21.5 cm x 28 cm (8½ in. x 11 in.). Fold each paper in half. Put one aside.

2 On the folded edge of the other paper, mark two dots, each one 4 cm (1½ in.) from the ends.

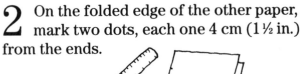

3 Starting at the dots, draw two large curved lines. The curved lines should go no further than 6 cm (2¼ in.) from the folded edge.

4 Under the top curved line, draw five more curved lines, each about 1 cm (⅜ in.) apart.

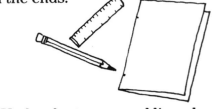

5 Starting above the bottom curved line, draw five more curved lines. There will now be six top curved lines and six bottom curved lines. The lines should not touch each other.

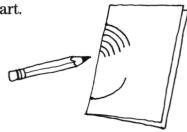

6 Cut all of the lines, starting from the folded edge.

7 Fold the middle section to the right. Remove this section by cutting along the fold line.

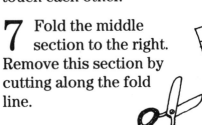

8 Fold to the right the second and fourth strips in the top section and bottom section, as shown.

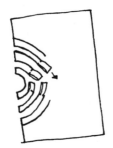

9 Cut out the strips that have been folded back.

10 Fold the entire inside section forward. Fold it back to its original position.

11 Open your paper and hold it like a tent. Push the cut section down in the opposite direction of the fold, so that the bars are pushed through to the other side of your paper. Close your paper with the cut section inside and press firmly. Open your paper. The mask will stand out.

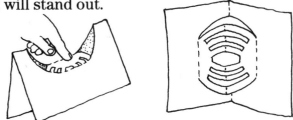

12 Take the paper that you put aside. Place it under the mask and with a pencil, lightly mark the areas for eyes, a nose and a mouth.

13 Remove the pop-up mask and put it aside. On the other sheet of paper, draw and colour eyes, a nose and a mouth at the marked places. You can also add hair and an outline for the face.

14 Apply glue to the back of your "mask" paper. Glue it to the paper on which you have drawn the face, which now becomes the outside paper. *Do not apply glue in the area of the mask.*

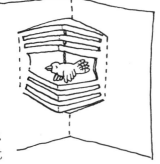

15 Now add details to your figure. You can add a uniform below the mask.

Other Ideas
Bird in a Cage

Make a bird cage the same way you made the mask but use heavy paper and make the spacing between the top and bottom bars smaller. Draw, colour and cut out a small bird. Tape a short piece of string to the back of the bird, then tape or tie the top of the string to the top bar. You may have to glue the top bar to the paper to support the bird.

More Pop-ups within Pop-ups

Draw a pop-up shape, then draw and cut lines inside it. Neither the pop-up shape nor the lines should go farther than the middle of the page. To push your pop-up through to the other side of the paper, follow steps 10 and 11 on page 17.

With these two ideas, you'll want every other bar to stick out. To do this, bend back every second strip and cut it off. Push these strips back, as in step 8 on page 16.

Skeleton

Valentine Heart

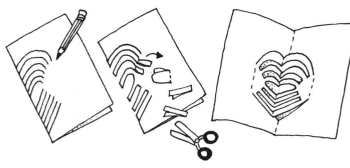

You can cut out sections in the middle of a pop-up shape.

Window

Mirror

Make a Dragon That
Turns into a Bird

1 Take two different coloured pieces of paper, each 21.5 cm x 28 cm (8½ in. x 11 in.). Fold each paper in half. Put one aside.

2 Place the other paper so that the folded edge is on your left. Mark a dot 8 cm (3⅛ in.) from the bottom of the paper.

3 From this dot, draw a curved line as shown.

4 From the end of the curved line, draw a diagonal dotted line towards the folded edge of the paper. The diagonal dotted line should not reach as far as the top edge of the paper.

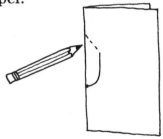

5 Cut the curved line. *Do not cut the dotted line.*

6 Fold the cut piece up along the dotted line. Press the fold firmly. Fold the cut piece down to its original position again.

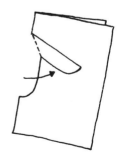
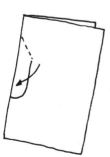

7 Open your paper and hold it like a tent. Push the cut piece down in the opposite direction of the fold, so that it is pushed through to the other side of the paper. Close the paper and press firmly. When you open your paper, a dragon's snout will pop out.

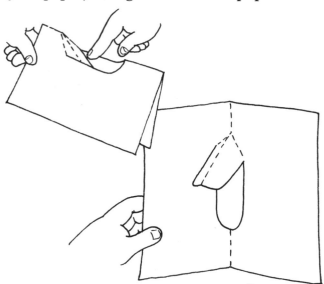

8 Draw a dragon with its eyes just above the snout and its body to the right of the snout.

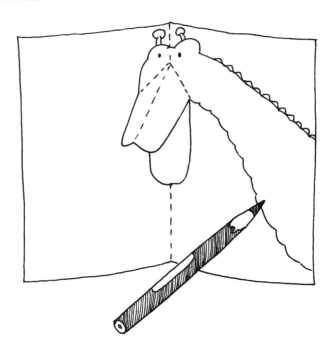

9 Add details by drawing on nostrils and scales. To make teeth, cut out small triangles of paper. Fold the bottoms of the triangles to create tabs. Apply glue to the tabs and place them along the inside edge of the snout.

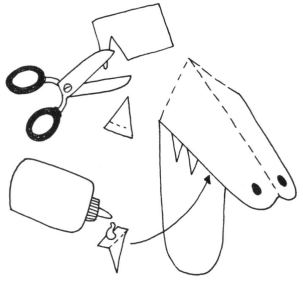

To turn the dragon into a bird when you hold the paper upside-down:

10 Draw, colour and cut out a red paper feather. Apply glue to the end of the feather and place it under the bottom of the snout. The feather becomes fire coming from the dragon's mouth.

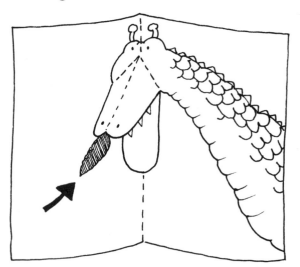

11 To make a horn for the dragon, take a piece of paper 7 cm x 7 cm (2¾ in. x 2¾ in.). Fold it in half. Draw a triangle shape as shown and cut it out.

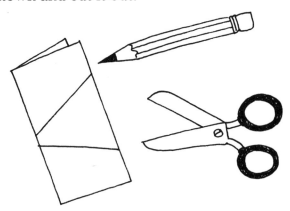

12 Fold back the bottom edges of the shape in opposite directions to create tabs. Apply glue to the bottom of the tabs and inside the horn. Match the folds of the tabs with the fold of the snout and place the horn just above the nostrils.

13 If you turn your dragon upside-down, you will see a bird. The nostrils become eyes and the horn becomes a beak!

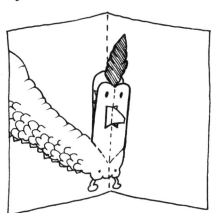

14 Apply glue to the back of your paper. Glue it on the paper you put aside. *Make sure that you do not apply glue in the area of the pop-up section.*

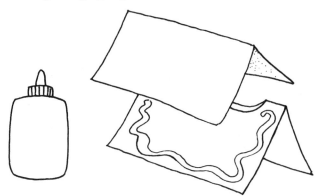

Other Ideas

Instead of making a dragon, make a boy with a baseball cap.

the boy's face will be the colour of the outside paper

Read a Good Book

1 Take two different coloured pieces of paper, each 21.5 cm x 28 cm (8½ in. x 11 in.). Fold each paper in half. Put one aside.

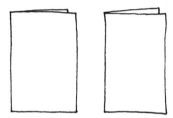

2 Place the other paper so that the folded edge is on your left. From the folded edge, draw two curved lines. This will be the head of the reader.

3 From the folded edge, draw two more curved lines as shown. These lines will be the reader's arms. Make sure that no lines reach beyond the middle of the page, which is 7 cm (2 ¾ in.) from the folded edge.

4 Cut all of the lines, starting at the folded edge. Fold the cut sections forward and then fold them back to their original positions.

5 Open your paper and hold it like a tent. Push the cut sections through to the other side of your paper. Close the paper and press firmly. Open to see the pop-up head and arms.

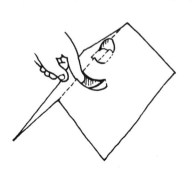
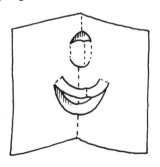

6 Complete the head by drawing and colouring a face and hair.

7 Draw lines from the head to the pop-up arms and draw in the rest of the body. Draw hands in the middle of the pop-up strip arms.

8 Draw, colour and cut out a small book that is 5 cm x 2.5 cm (2 in. x 1 in.). Fold it in half. Decorate it and write a title **on the top** half of the book.

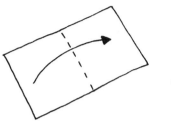

9 Apply glue to the bottom half of the book as shown. Place the book behind the hands, so that the folds match.

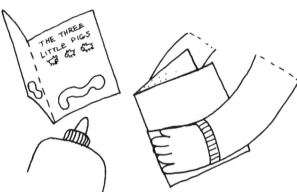

10 Apply glue to the back of **your paper.** Glue it on the paper you put aside, which now becomes the outside **paper.** *Make sure that you do not apply glue in the area of the pop-up sections.*

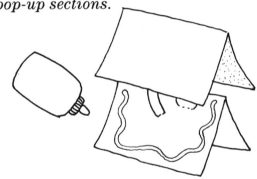

11 Now decorate the inside and outside papers. This idea would be very good for a reading or library display.

Other Ideas

Thank-you Card

Write your thank-you note on the book.

Gift Card

Put a small, light gift, such as a ring, inside the book. Make sure the gift fits within one side of the fold.

Make a Bird Fly

1 Take two pieces of paper, each 21.5 cm x 28 cm (8½ in. x 11 in.). They can be different colours. Fold each paper in half. Put one aside.

2 Place the other paper so that the folded edge is on your left. From the folded edge, draw two curved lines as shown. The lines should not reach beyond 6 cm (2¼ in.) from the folded edge.

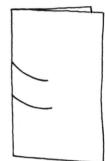

3 Cut the two lines, starting from the folded edge.

4 Fold the cut strip forward and then fold it back to its original position.

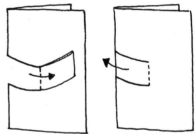

5 Open your paper and hold it like a tent. Push the strip through to the other side of your paper. Close the paper and press firmly, then open it to see the pop-up wings.

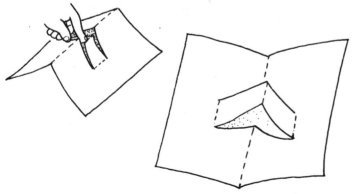

6 To make the body parts of the bird, take another piece of paper 11 cm x 28 cm (4¼ in. x 11 in.). Use paper that is the same colour as the paper with the pop-up wings. Fold it in half.

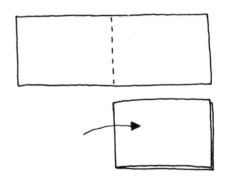

7 Place the paper so that the folded edge is on your left. Draw half of a bird's body on the folded edge of the paper, as shown.

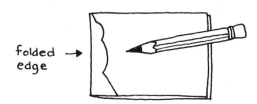

folded edge →

8 Draw wings on the open edge of the paper as shown.

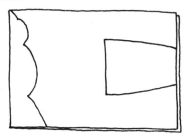

9 Cut out the body and wings. Fold the narrow edge of each wing to create tabs. Cut fringes in the wings to make feathers. Cut a fringe in the tail of the body.

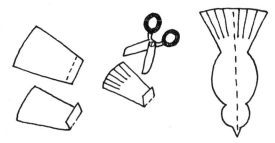

10 Apply glue to the underside of the fold of the pop-up wings from step 5. Place the body of the bird under the fold so that the folds match. The head should be facing the bottom of the page.

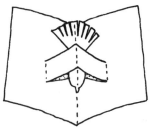

11 Apply glue to the tabs of the wing feathers. Place the tabs on the edge of each pop-up wing so that the folds line up. You may have to trim the tabs to match the ends of the pop-up wings.

12 Apply glue to the back of your paper. Glue it to the paper you put aside, which now becomes the outside paper. *Make sure you do not apply glue in the area of the pop-up wings.*

13 Now decorate the inside and outside papers. Colour your bird or add small paper feathers.

Other Ideas
Butterfly

Add two more wing pieces, a body and antennae to make a butterfly.

Make an Albatross

1 Take two pieces of paper the same colour, each 21.5 cm x 28 cm (8½ in. x 11 in.). Fold each paper in half. Take a piece of paper that is the same size but another colour. Fold it in half and put it aside.

2 Place one of the first two pieces of paper on top of the other, so that the folded edges are on your left.

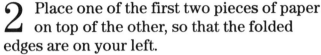

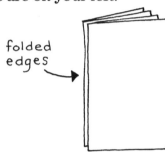

3 On the top paper, mark a dot 8 cm (3⅛ in.) from the bottom of the paper. From this dot, draw a curved line upwards, so that it ends about 7 cm (2¾ in.) higher than the dot, as shown.

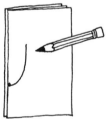

4 Mark a dot on the folded edge 4 cm (1½ in.) from the top of the paper. Draw a dotted line from the dot to the end of the curved line, as shown.

5 Carefully hold both pieces of paper so that they line up exactly. Cut the curved line, starting from the folded edge. Make sure that you are cutting through both folded papers. *Do not cut the dotted line.*

6 With the papers together, fold both cut sections up along the dotted line. Fold the sections down to the original position again.

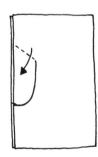

7 Separate the papers. Open one and hold it like a tent. Push the cut piece down in the opposite direction of the fold, so that it is pushed through to the other side of the paper. Close your paper with the cut section inside and press firmly. When you open your paper, a bird's beak will pop out. Repeat this with the other paper.

8 Take one of the papers and close it. Place it so that the folded edge is on your left. Match the other paper to it, placing one on top of the other.

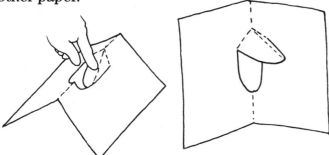

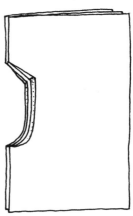

9 Now flip over the paper on top, so that the folded edges are still together.

10 With a pencil, trace along the inside of the cut section of the top paper onto the bottom paper. Remove the top paper and cut out the section you have drawn.

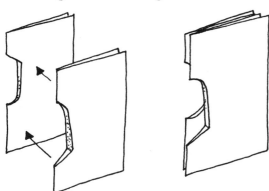

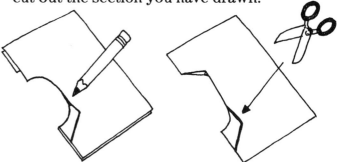

11 Open both papers. Place one paper over the other as shown so that there is a top and bottom beak.

12 Glue the two papers together. *Do not apply glue in the area of the beaks.*

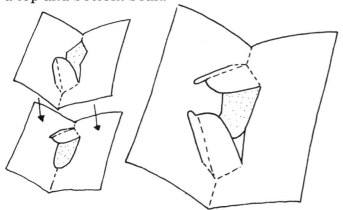

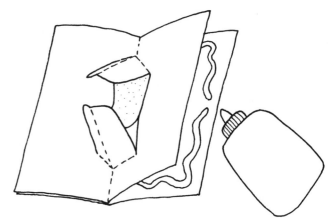

13 Glue the paper you put aside to the back of the other two papers. *Do not apply glue in the area of the beaks.* This becomes the outside paper.

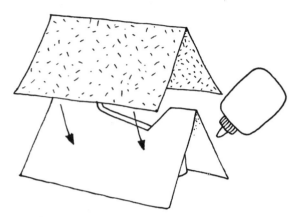

14 To make a bird, draw a curved line down from the left side of the mouth then up to the right side of the mouth. Draw and colour eyes, feathers and a neck.

15 Decorate the inside and outside papers. For the best pop-up action, hold the bottom corners of the papers when you open and close them.

Other Ideas

A Different Beak

Make a fold at the end of each beak. Push in the middle of the fold to create a triangle shape.

Make a Big Bear Hug

By cutting one fold and adding another shaped piece of paper, you can create many unusual mouths.

1 Take two pieces of paper, each 21.5 cm x 28 cm (8½ in. x 11 in.). Fold each paper in half. Put one aside.

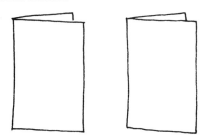

2 To make the bear's lower jaw, start by putting a dot in approximately the centre of the folded edge.

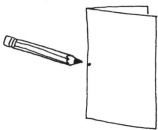

3 From this dot, draw a jagged curved line as shown. *Do not draw past the middle of the page.*

4 Cut on the line, starting from the folded edge.

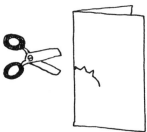

5 Fold the flap forward and down. Then fold it back to its original position.

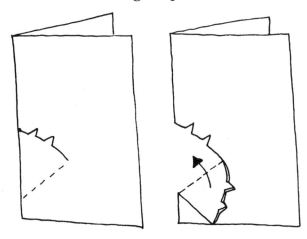

6 Hold your paper like a tent. Put your finger on the cut section and push down in the opposite direction of the fold, so that the cut section is pushed through to the other side of the paper. Close your paper and press firmly.

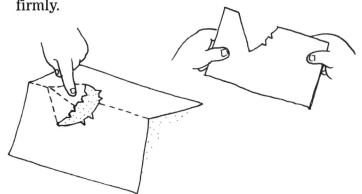

7 To make the upper jaw, trace the shape below onto a piece of paper. With a pencil, lightly trace the dotted lines.

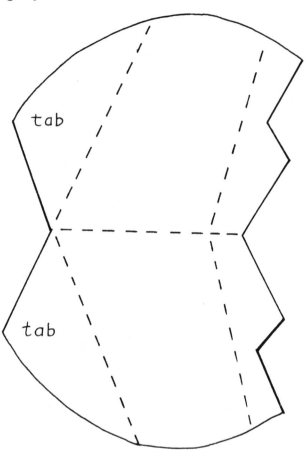

8 Cut out the shape. Fold along the dotted lines so that the pointed parts are standing up.

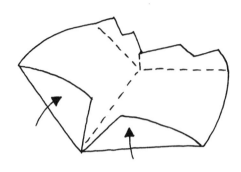

9 Apply glue on the bottom of each tab.

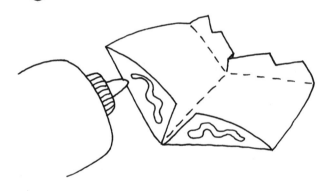

10 Fit this cut shape onto the area above the pop-up bottom jaw, so that the teeth are facing down. Glue the tabs down, so that the fold line of the upper jaw lines up with the fold line of the teeth.

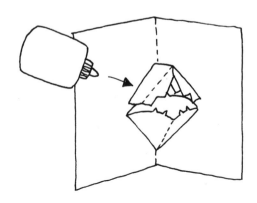

11 Draw and colour a face around your mouth.

12 Apply glue to the back of your paper. Glue it to the paper you put aside, which now becomes the outside paper. *Do not apply glue in the area of the pop-up mouth.*

13 Decorate the inside and outside papers.

I WANT TO GIVE YOU A

GREAT BIG

BEAR HUG

Other Ideas

You can make many types of faces by using different upper jaw shapes. Try these:

lion

pterodactyl

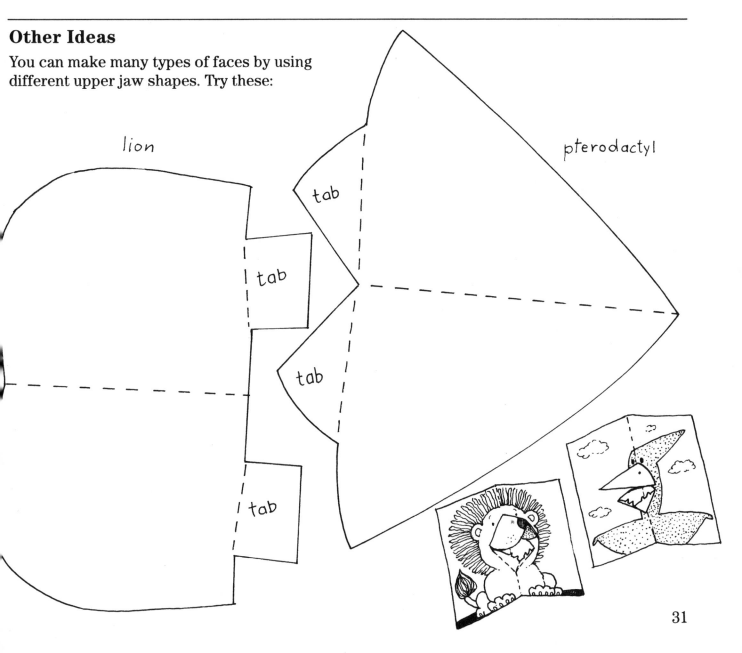

tab

tab

tab

tab

tab

Make More Animals Using Cut Shapes

The three steps below tell you how to glue any animal head in place. You can make a cow following the instructions here or create any pop-up animal you like.

To make sure your pop-up folds flat, follow these instructions when gluing the animal's head to the page.

1 Apply glue to the back of the left ear and place it on the left side of your paper. Position the ear so that it is completely inside the left half of the page.

2 Apply glue to the back of the right ear. Close your paper and press firmly. The right ear will now be glued to the right side of your paper. Allow the glue to dry.

3 When you open your paper, the animal's face will be standing out.

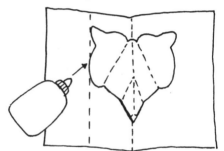

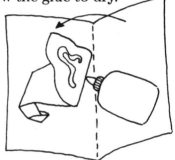

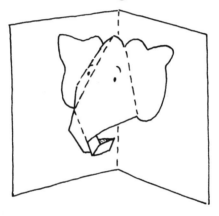

Make a Cow

1 Take two pieces of paper 21.5 cm x 28 cm (8½ in. x 11 in.). Fold them in half. Place them so that the folded edges are on your left.

2 On one folded page, draw the shape shown below, including the dotted lines. Cut it out. Score and fold along the dotted lines. This is the upper jaw and face.

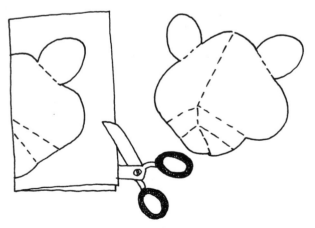

3 Apply glue to the area shown. Pinch along the fold lines and press the glued areas together.

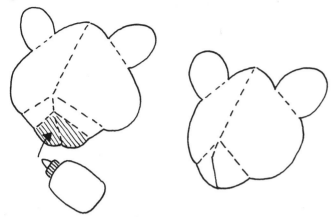

4 On the other folded page, draw and cut out this shape. This is the lower jaw.

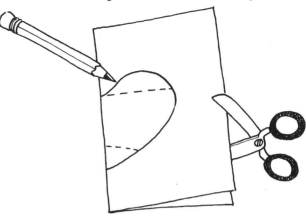

5 Fold along the dotted lines to create the shape shown below.

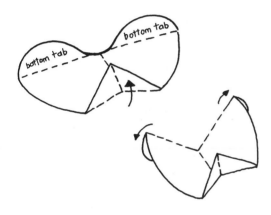

6 Take a piece of heavy paper 30 cm x 23 cm (12 in. x 9 in.). This will be your outside paper. Follow the instructions on page 32 to glue the upper jaw into the outside paper.

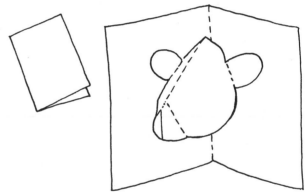

7 To attach the lower jaw to the outside paper, apply glue to the bottom tabs. Place the lower jaw under the upper jaw, matching fold lines.

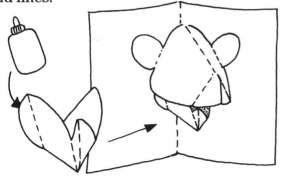

8 Cut out horns and glue them to the top part of the head. Decorate the inside and outside papers.

Part Two **Super Structures**

If you want to make soaring city skyscrapers or a medieval castle, then super structures are for you. Start by cutting and folding a paper base, then let your imagination take over! Just follow the directions and add parts you make from paper or whatever you like to create incredible super pop-ups.

With some of these ideas, you'll be building your paper base in the middle of the page. With others, such as the skyscrapers, you'll discover how to attach large bases around your page.

Another super structure you'll find here includes adding a post to the middle of your pop-up. The post shoots in and out of your structure when you open and close the page, so you can make a volcano that erupts, Pinocchio and his growing nose – or anything you can think of!

Tips

- When you attach a structure to the base paper, make sure you allow the glue to dry before you carefully open the paper to see your figure pop up.
- If you are frustrated with your structure because it does not close properly, don't give up! Carefully loosen the glued areas and try placing the folded piece more carefully.
- If you're working with a figure that has a V-shaped base, make sure the middle of the base is placed directly on the fold line of your paper.
- When you add parts to a base, make sure they do not stick outside of your base paper when the paper is folded shut.
- If you wish to build bigger structures, use a bigger or heavier base paper.

Make an Awesome Insect

1 Fold in half a piece of heavy paper (such as construction paper), 30 cm x 23 cm (12 in. x 9 in.). Put it aside. This will be your base paper.

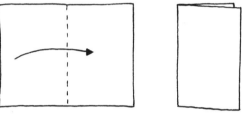

3 Cut a 1 cm (⅜ in.) piece off both ends of your strip.

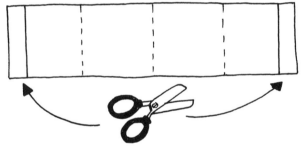

5 Open the cube so that the peaks of the folds face up. Apply glue to both end sections of the strip.

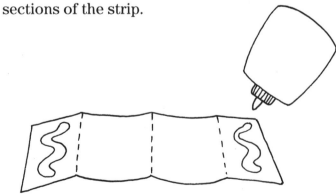

2 Cut a strip of paper, 4 cm x 16 cm (1 ½ in. x 6 ¼ in.). Fold the strip in half end to end. Then fold the strip in half again. Open the strip and you will have three folds.

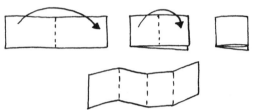

4 Use mountain folds (see page 6) to fold the strip along the fold lines you created in step 2. You will now have a cube shape.

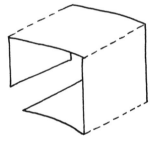

6 Fold the strip into a cube again. Place the cube in the centre of your paper, an equal distance from the top and bottom. Line up the middle fold in the strip with the fold in your paper. The ends of the strip should not touch at the middle of the paper. Make sure that your paper opens and closes easily.

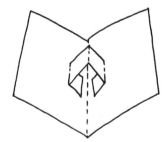

7 To make your insect, use interesting paper such as coloured foil, gift wrap or brightly coloured paper. Draw and cut out three circles of paper with a diameter of 6 cm (2¼ in.) for the body parts. The circles can be different colours.

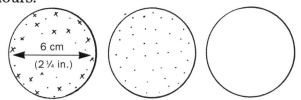

8 Fold the circles in half. Apply glue to the back of one circle and place it on the middle of the cube. Match the fold lines of the circle with the fold lines of the cube.

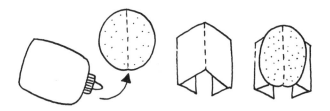

9 Apply a small amount of glue to the top and bottom of the circle, on the fold line. Attach the other two circles so that their fold lines match the fold lines of the first circle.

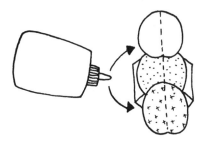

10 To make eyes, fold a piece of paper 8 cm x 5 cm (3⅛ in. x 2 in.) in half. Draw a spiral on it and cut it out. You will have two spirals. Apply glue to the back of each spiral and place them on the top of the upper circle. Cut out small eyeballs and glue them to the spirals.

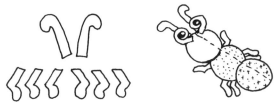

11 Draw and cut out six legs and two antennae. Glue them to the body as shown. Make sure that the legs do not get folded when you close your paper.

12 To make the wings, take a piece of paper, 23 cm x 17 cm (9 in. x 7 in.). Fold it in half. Along the open edge, draw and cut out two large wings and two smaller wings.

13 Make a fold about 1 cm (⅜ in.) from the small end of the large wings to create a tab. Apply glue to the back of each tab and press the wings to the body as shown.

14 To make supports for the large wings, take two strips of heavy paper, 6 cm x 1 cm (2¼ in. x ⅜ in.). Fold the strips into thirds so that each section is 2 cm (¾ in.) long.

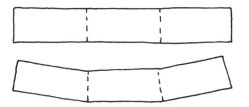

15 Hold one folded strip so that the ends point to the right. Apply glue to the top section of the strip and press it to the underside of the left wing, near the outside edge.

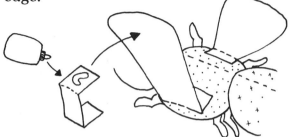

16 Apply glue to the bottom section of the strip. Close the left side of the page and press firmly.

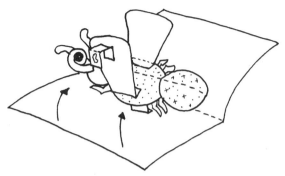

17 Hold the other strip so that the ends point to the left. Attach it to the right wing as in steps 15 and 16. When you open the paper, the wings will be supported by the strips.

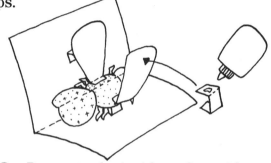

18 Apply glue to the straight ends of the small wings. Place them on the insect's body below the large wings. They should be close to the body of the insect.

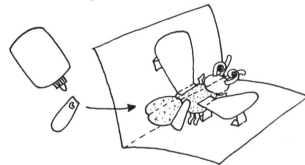

19 Decorate the inside and outside papers.

Other Ideas

Robot

Make a robot by gluing square pieces of paper to the cube. Add details such as antennae, dials and a face.

Make an Alien from Outer Space

1 Fold in half a piece of heavy paper, 21.5 cm x 28 cm (8½ in. x 11 in.). Put it aside. This will be your base paper.

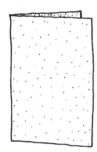

2 Take another piece of paper 21.5 cm x 28 cm (8½ in. x 11 in.) that is a different colour. Fold it in half and place it so that the folded edge is on your left.

3 Mark a dot on the folded edge 15 cm (6 in.) up from the bottom of the paper. Mark a second dot 10 cm (4 in.) along the bottom of the paper to the right of the fold.

4 Between these two dots, draw the following shape. Mark the dotted line as well. Cut out the shape.

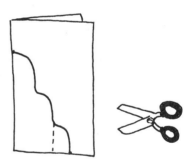

5 Fold along the dotted line to create a valley fold (see page 6). Bend the folded section to the left.

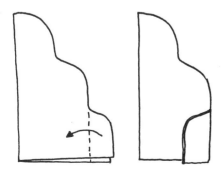

6 On the right folded edge of the shape, draw a line 2 cm (¾ in.) long as shown. Cut the line.

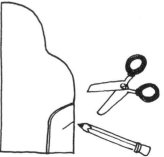

7 Fold the cut section forward and press firmly. Fold the cut section back to its original position.

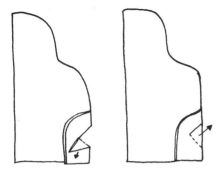

8 Open your large shape. Bend the middle fold to create a mountain fold (see page 6). Bend the side folds to create valley folds. You now have two side flaps.

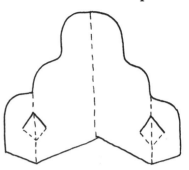

9 To make the small cut sections pop out, pull the shapes towards you and press along the fold lines. The cut diamond shapes will stand out towards you.

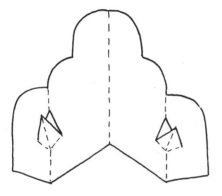

10 Fold the large shape together again. Apply glue to the back of the left flap and place it on the left side of your paper as shown. *Do not apply glue on the "diamond cuts."* Press firmly and allow it to dry.

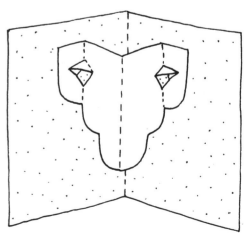

11 Apply glue to the back of the right flap. Close your paper and press firmly. The right flap will now be glued to the right side of your paper. Allow the glue to dry.

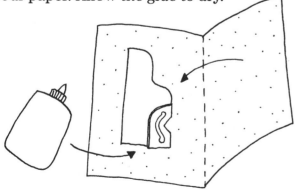

12 Open your paper and flip it over as shown. The face will be standing out.

13 To make eyes, fold a piece of paper 5 cm x 10 cm (2 in. x 4 in.) in half. Draw and cut out a circle. When you separate the paper, you will have two circles.

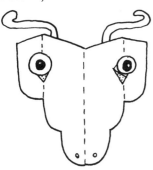

14 Apply glue to half of the pop-up eye sections as shown. Place the circles on these sections and press firmly.

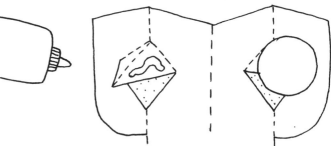

15 Add further decorations such as eyeballs, antennae and nostrils.

16 If you wish, cut two small spirals, the same size as the eyes. To attach them, glue the middle section of each spiral to the end of the nose.

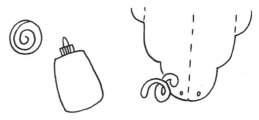

17 Apply glue to the front of the tip of one of the spirals. Close your card, press it together and allow it to dry. When you open the card, the end of the spiral will be glued in place. Repeat this step with the other spiral.

18 Decorate the inside and outside papers.

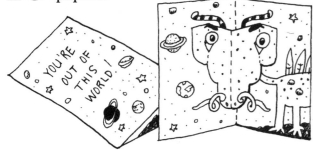

Other Ideas

Person Holding a Sign

Make two arms and glue them to the pop-up diamond shapes. Tape a piece of string between them and attach two small signs to the string as shown. Add a head and feet.

Make Skyscrapers

 **1** Fold in half a piece of construction paper or light Bristol board, 30 cm x 23 cm (12 in. x 9 in.). This will be your base paper.

2 To make the first skyscraper, fold in half a piece of construction paper or heavy paper, 16 cm x 10 cm (6¼ in. x 4 in.).

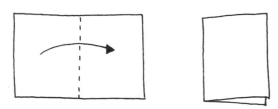

3 Open it and fold the bottom edge up 1.2 cm (½ in.).

4 Fold the bottom edge down to its original position. Mark with a dot the spot where the fold lines meet. Draw a little triangle with the dot at its top and cut it out. You now have two tabs at the bottom of the skyscraper.

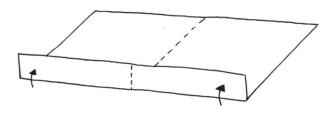

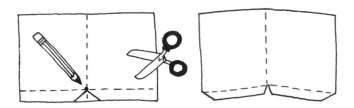

5 Turn your skyscraper over and draw on windows, doors, etc.

6 Apply glue to the front of the left tab and then place the left side of your skyscraper face down on the base paper as shown. Press firmly.

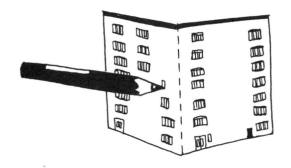

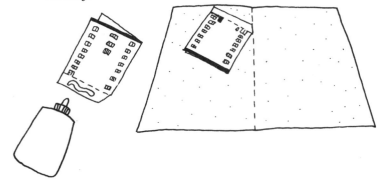

7 Apply glue to the front of the right tab and close your paper. Press the paper firmly for about a minute.

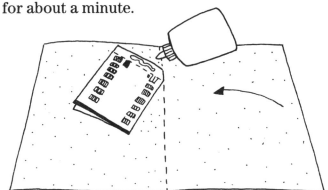

8 Open the paper and you will see a skyscraper standing up.

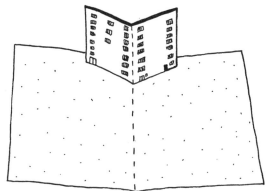

9 Measure and cut four strips of paper, 12 cm x 1 cm (4¾ in. x ⅜ in.). Fold each one in half end to end. Fold each in half again so that it is folded in quarters. Put the strips aside.

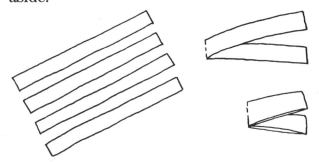

10 To add two skyscrapers, cut two heavy pieces of paper, each 9 cm x 6 cm (3½ in. x 2¼ in.). Draw and colour windows, doors and other details.

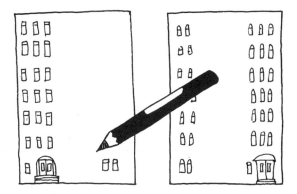

11 Open one of the small strips. Put glue on both end sections of the strip.

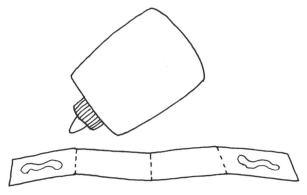

12 Fold the strip into a cube shape. Place it in the middle of the bottom edge of the left side of the skyscraper, so that one end is glued to the skyscraper and the other is glued to the base paper.

13 Repeat the last two steps, gluing a folded strip on the right side of the skyscraper. Close your paper to make sure that your strips fold properly.

14 Apply glue to the front of the left strip. Attach one of the buildings from step 10 to the glued strip. Repeat this with the right strip.

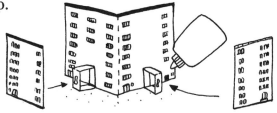

15 To make another set of buildings, cut out two heavy pieces of paper, each 5 cm x 5 cm (2 in. x 2 in.). Draw and colour windows, doors and other details.

16 Take the other two folded strips. Fold them into cubes and glue them to the front middle area of each building as shown.

17 Apply glue to the front of the left strip. Place a building on the glued strip. Repeat this with the right strip. Close your paper and press firmly.

18 If any part sticks out from your paper, cut it shorter. Decorate the inside and outside papers.

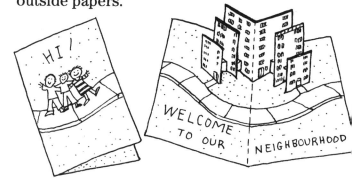

Other Ideas

Castle

The back building is a castle and the front pieces can be bushes and knights.

Make a Boat

1 Take two pieces of heavy paper, each 30 cm x 23 cm (12 in. x 9 in.). Fold each paper in half. Put both aside.

2 Take another piece of paper, 21.5 cm x 28 cm (8½ in. x 11 in.). Fold it in half top to bottom. Fold it again so that it is folded in quarters. Fold again so that it is folded in eighths.

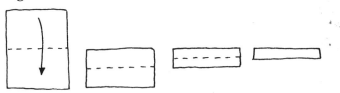

3 Open your paper and fold it in half lengthways as shown.

4 Open the paper and along the right edge, mark sections 1 to 8 with a pencil.

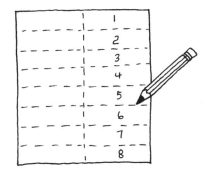

5 Cut off half of sections 1 and 2, 4 and 5, 7 and 8 as shown. Do not cut out 3 and 6.

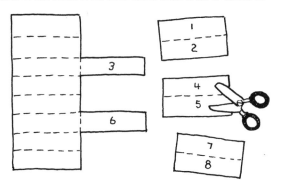

6 Fold your piece of paper so that each fold is a mountain fold (see page 6).

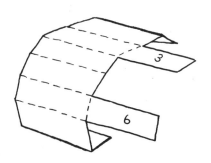

45

7 Apply glue to sections 1 and 2. Bend them around and under sections 7 and 8 and press them together firmly.

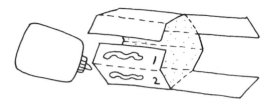

8 Fold out the two side pieces. These are your tabs. Pinch your fold lines at the ends so that you have a hexagonal shape.

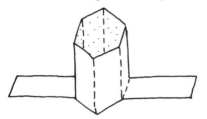

9 Open up one of the pieces of paper from step 1.

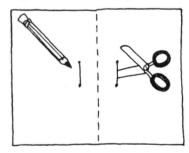

10 Place your hexagonal shape in the middle of the paper, matching the fold line to the ends of the shape. Mark dots on the paper at the inside edge of each tab, as shown.

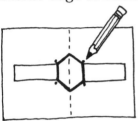

11 Remove the hexagonal shape. Draw vertical lines between the dots. With a knife or sharp scissors, cut the two lines.

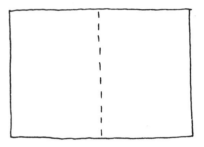

12 Insert the tabs of the hexagonal shape into the two cut lines. Apply glue to the top of each tab and press the tabs to the bottom of the paper.

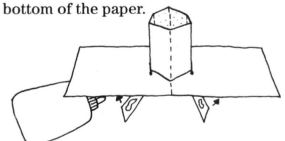

13 Close your paper and press firmly. When you open it, you should have a standing hexagonal structure.

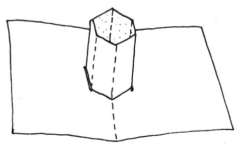

14 Fold a piece of paper 21.5 cm x 11 cm (8½ in. x 4¼ in.) in half lengthways as shown. Place it so that the folded edge is on the left. Draw a boat shape on the open edge as shown. Cut it out. You will have two separate shapes which will be the sides of your boat.

15 Apply glue to the outside of the hexagonal structure just above the tabs.

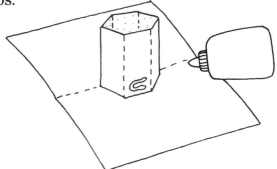

16 Place one side of the boat against one glued area. Repeat with the other side of the boat.

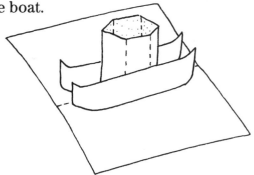

17 Staple or tape the ends of the boat together at each end.

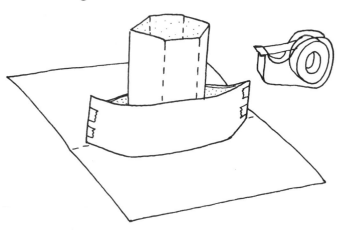

18 **Optional** To close in the top of the boat, take a piece of paper 3 cm x 10 cm (1⅛ in. x 4 in.) and fold it in half. Apply glue to each end and place the ends inside the hexagonal structure as shown. Push the middle of the strip down so that it is level with the top of the boat.

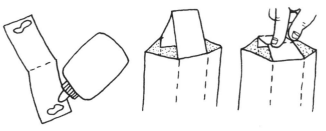

19 Apply glue to the back of your paper. Glue it to the paper you put aside, which now becomes the outside paper. Decorate the boat with portholes, doors and flags. Do not put a flag at the top of the boat or it will stick out of your paper. Decorate the outside paper as well.

AHOY MATE! YOU'RE INVITED TO A PARTY

Other Ideas

Wishing Well

Follow steps 2 to 13 using paper 11 cm x 28 cm (4¼ in. x 11 in.). For the roof, fold in half a piece of paper, 14 cm x 10 cm (5½ in. x 4 in.). Glue it to the hexagonal structure as shown. Make a small pail to hang inside the well.

WISH YOU WERE HERE!

Make a Holiday Tree

1 Fold in half a heavy piece of paper, 21.5 cm x 28 cm (8½ in. x 11 in.). This will be your base paper.

2 Fold in half a green piece of paper, 21.5 cm x 28 cm (8½ in. x 11 in.).

3 Place the green paper so that the folded edge is on your left. Draw a tree along the folded edge. Cut it out.

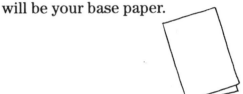

4 Cut out three strips of heavy paper, each 7.5 cm x 2.5 cm (3 in. x 1 in.).

5 Measure 2.5 cm (1 in.) from the left side of one strip. Fold at this line. From this fold, measure 2.5 cm (1 in.). Fold at this line. You will have a strip folded into thirds. Repeat these steps with the other two strips.

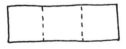

6 Hold one folded strip so that the ends are on the right. Apply glue to the bottom of one end. Place it along the right side of the fold line in the middle of the paper.

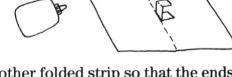

7 Apply glue to the top section of the strip. Place the folded tree on the glued area so that the fold line of the tree matches the fold line of the strip. Make sure that the tree doesn't stick out beyond your base paper.

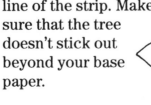

8 Hold another folded strip so that the ends are to the left. Apply glue to the bottom and place it in the middle of the folded tree as shown.

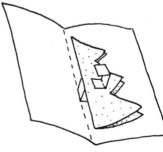

9 Apply glue to the top of the strip. Place it with the glued section facing up as shown. Close the left side of the paper and press firmly.

10 Place the folded tree on the left side of the paper. Hold the third folded strip so that the ends are facing right. Apply glue to the bottom of the folded strip.

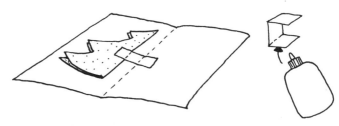

11 Place it in the middle area of the tree and press firmly.

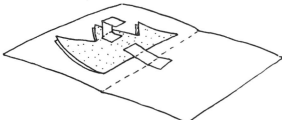

12 Apply glue to the end of the strip. Close the right side of the paper and press firmly. When you open your paper, you will have a pop-up tree.

13 Decorate your tree. If you wish, glue presents to the base of the tree.

14 To make a child behind the tree, colour and cut out a figure. Cut a line halfway up your figure. Cut a line halfway down the tops of the folded strips, as shown. Slide the two cut lines together. You can make a figure for the other side of the tree as well, or attach a message.

15 Decorate the inside and outside papers.

HAPPY HOLIDAYS

49

Make a Castle

You may photocopy the patterns for this pop-up or trace them on graph paper. Follow these symbols when tracing.

———————— = cutting line

– – – – – – = mountain folds (see page 6)

·················· = valley folds (see page 6)

1 Fold in half a heavy piece of paper, 30 cm x 23 cm (12 in. x 9 in.), and put it aside. This will be your base paper.

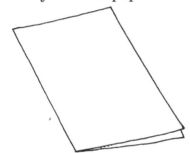

2 Take a piece of graph paper, 21.5 cm x 28 cm (8½ in. x 11 in.) with squares that are approximately .6 cm x .6 cm (¼ in. x ¼ in.).

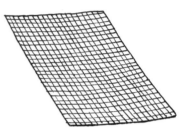

3 Trace the diagrams on page 51 on the graph paper. See the symbols above. (If you wish, use different colours for the different lines.) Or photocopy the diagrams.

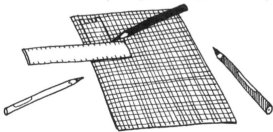

4 Cut along the solid lines. Fold the dot and dash lines to create mountain folds and valley folds (see page 6).

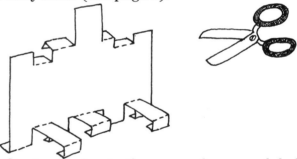

5 Colour the castle. You may wish to cut small windows out of the main building, using a cutting blade (ask an adult for help).

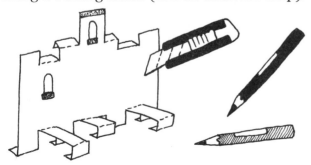

6 Apply glue to the rows of squares labelled "glue 1" as shown.

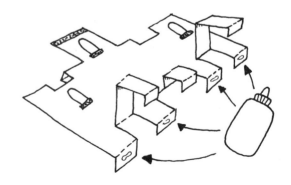

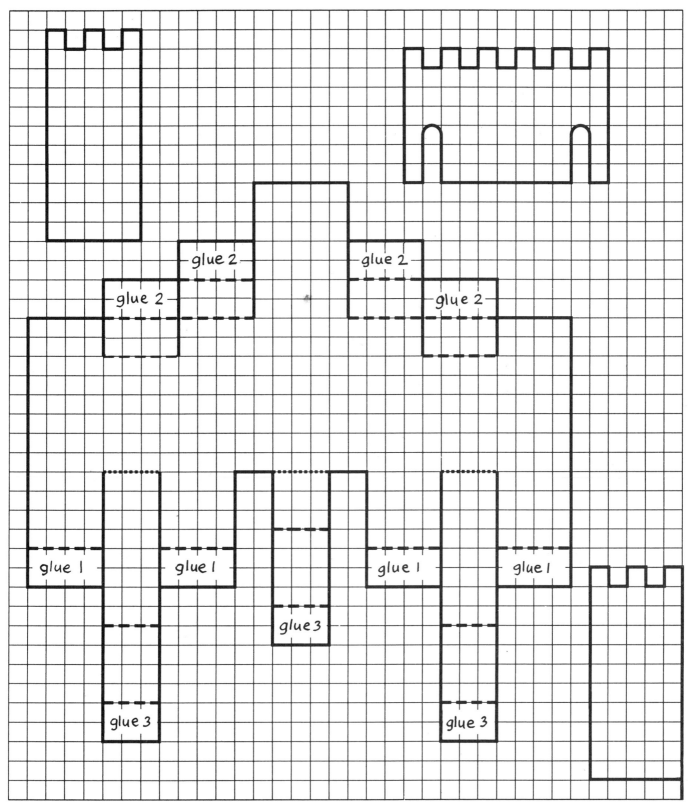

glue 2

glue 2

glue 2

glue 2

glue 1

glue 1

glue 1

glue 1

glue 3

glue 3

glue 3

7 Open the base paper and place the castle along the fold line. The glued areas should be against the fold line.

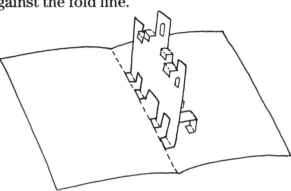

8 Apply glue to the squares labelled "glue 2."

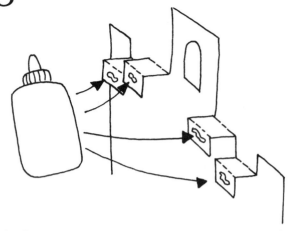

9 Close the left side of the page and press firmly. The back of the castle will be attached to the left side of the page.

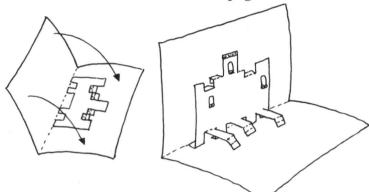

10 Fold the three front sections back as shown. Apply glue to the squares marked "glue 3."

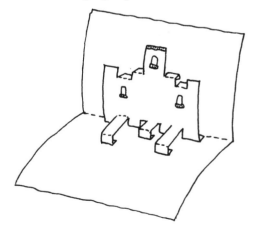

11 Close the right side of the page and press firmly. The front three sections will now be attached to the right side of the page.

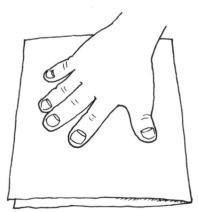

12 When you open your paper, you will have a pop-up castle.

13 Now cut out the remaining sections that you have drawn on the graph paper.

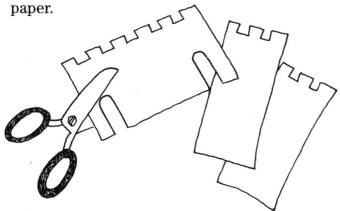

14 Apply glue to the front of each long folded strip. Attach a tall tower to each glued section.

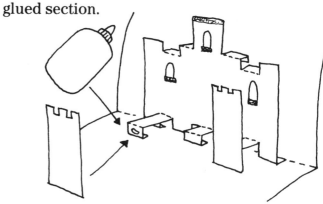

15 Apply glue to the front of the short folded strip. Attach the short tower to this strip.

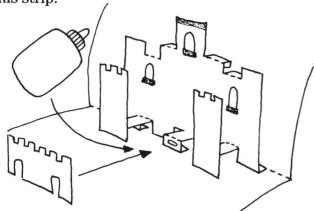

16 Decorate the castle with flags and soldiers. You may wish to add an interesting background.

You're the king of our castle!

17 Decorate the outside paper.

HAPPY FATHER'S DAY DAD!!

Other Ideas

Add Some Action

You can add people or animals on sliding strips along the front of the castle to create an action scene.

Pull ▶

53

Make Pinocchio's Nose Grow

1 Take one heavy piece of paper 30 cm x 23 cm (12 in. x 9 in.) and fold it in half. Put it aside. This is your base paper.

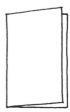

2 To make the nose, take a heavy piece of paper 28 cm x 5 cm (11 in. x 2 in.) and fold it in half.

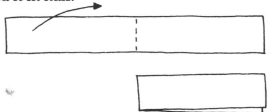

3 Take a Popsicle stick that is approximately 11 cm (4¼ in.) long. If you do not have a Popsicle stick, use a stiff piece of cardboard that is the same size. Open the folded strip. Apply glue to one side of the stick and place the tip of it near the folded edge of the paper as shown.

4 Apply glue to the top of the stick and close the top half of the paper over it. Press firmly.

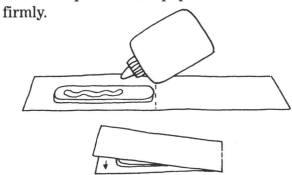

5 Make tabs by folding the bottom sections back as far as the stick.

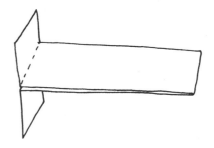

6 Starting at the folded edge, cut down along either side of the stick. Cut only as far as the end of the stick.

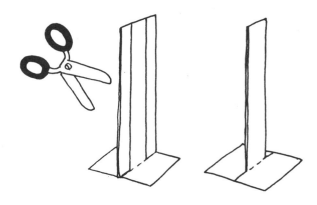

7 Apply glue to the bottom of the tabs and place on the base paper so that the tabs lie along the fold line of the paper. Press firmly.

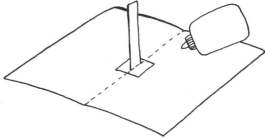

8 To make the face, draw a circle with a diameter of 15 cm (6 in.). (You can use a compass for this, if you have one.) Cut out the circle.

15 cm
(6 in.)

9 Draw a line from the centre of the circle to the edge of the circle. Cut this line.

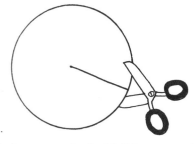

10 Overlap the cut edges by about 8 cm (3⅛ in.) and apply glue between the layers to create a cone shape.

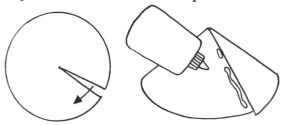

11 Fold the cone in half. Measure 1.6 cm (⅝ in.) down from the tip of the cone and draw a curved line around the cone at that point. Cut along the line. You will now have a hole at the tip of the cone.

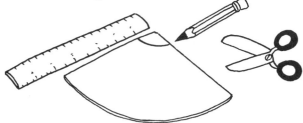

12 To make the ears, fold in half a piece of paper (the same colour as the cone) that is 10 cm x 5 cm (4 in. x 2 in.). Along the open edge, draw and cut out the following ear shape.

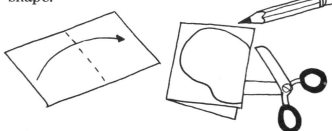

13 Create tabs on the ears by making a fold 2 cm (¾ in.) from the straight end.

14 Glue the ends of the tabs to the cone as shown. The ears should be directly opposite one another. Reinforce the tabs with tape.

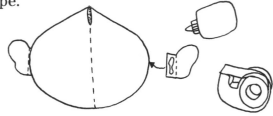

15 Draw a face on the cone. You can glue on wool for hair. Don't draw on a nose!

16 Place the cone over the stick, so that the stick is pushed through the hole. If necessary, trim the hole to make it bigger.

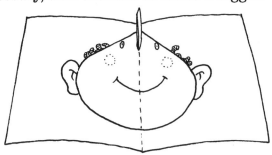

17 Match the fold lines of the cone to the fold lines of the paper. Apply glue under each ear. Pull the ears carefully outward so that they are an equal distance from the middle fold line. Press them firmly to the paper. If necessary, apply tape to the ears to secure them.

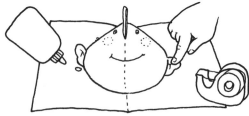

18 You now have a face with a nose poking through the middle of it. To make it work, close and open your paper. When you open the paper, Pinocchio's nose will grow. If it is not working properly, make sure that the hole is big enough for the stick.

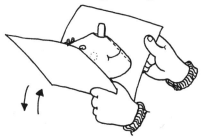

19 Decorate the inside and outside papers.

Other Ideas

Erupting Volcano

Cover the stick with red paper to make lava. Turn the cone into a mountain.

Make a Creepy, Crawly Crab

1 Take a heavy piece of paper 30 cm x 23 cm (12 in. x 9 in.) and fold it in half. Put it aside. This is your base paper.

2 Take another piece of paper 21.5 cm x 28 cm (8½ in. x 11 in.) that is a different colour from the base paper. You will be making the crab with this paper. Fold it in half and place it so that the folded edge is on your left.

3 Mark a dot on the folded edge 10 cm (4 in.) up from the bottom of the paper. Mark a second dot 12 cm (4¾ in.) along the bottom of the paper to the right of the fold. Draw a curved line between the dots as shown.

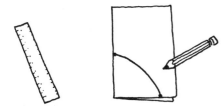

4 Cut along this line. Open the paper and you will have a curved shape. Fold the bottom edge up 1.2 cm (½ in.). Save the remaining paper.

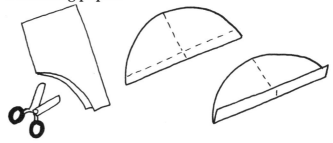

5 Fold the bottom edge back to its original position. Mark with a dot the spot where the fold lines meet. Draw a little triangle below the dot and cut it out. You now have two tabs at the bottom of the curved shape.

6 Place your base paper so that the fold line is on the left. On the fold line, mark a dot 11 cm (4¼ in.) from the bottom of the paper. Mark a second dot at the top of the paper 5 cm (2 in.) to the right of the fold. Draw a line between the two dots. Take the top left corner and fold it forward along the line. Open your paper and you will see a large triangle.

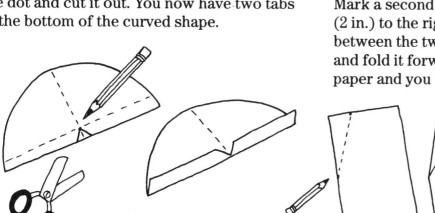

7 Now go back to your curved shape. Fold the bottom tabs in so that they meet in the centre (where you drew the dot). Apply glue to the bottom of both tabs.

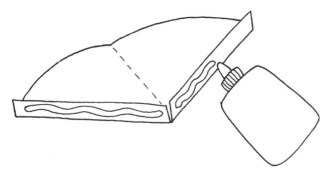

8 Fit the curved shape into the large triangle on your base paper. Glue the tabs of your shape down along the triangle lines of your base paper. The fold lines of the shape should line up with the fold lines of the base paper.

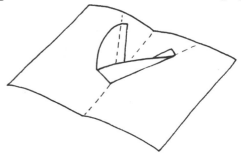

9 To make a head, fold in half a piece of paper, 5 cm x 5 cm (2 in. x 2 in.). Draw and cut out a half circle. Open it up.

10 Apply glue at the bottom of the circle. Place the circle on the top of the curved shape, so that the folds match and the top part of the head is above the curved shape. Make sure that the head doesn't show above the paper when it is closed.

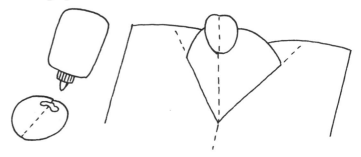

11 To make the arms, take the paper that was left from cutting the curved shape. Place it so that the folded edge is on the left. Mark a dot 2 cm (¾ in.) up from the bottom of the folded edge. Draw a curve as shown and cut it out. Cut along the fold line to divide the shape in two.

12 Fold the bottom edge of each arm to create tabs. Apply glue to the bottom of each tab and place them on the body as shown. Make sure that the arms are not folded when the paper is closed. If they are, cut the arms shorter or move the arms into a different position.

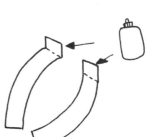

13 Add details such as claws, eyes on stalks and antennae. Make sure that paper parts are positioned so that nothing sticks out of your paper when it is closed.

14 Decorate the inside and outside papers.

Other Ideas

Creature from Outer Space

Create a creature by adding strange eyes, a mouth and arms.

Part Three **Super Slides and Turns**

Imagine making a face with changing eyeballs. Or how about a clown who juggles? When you make super slides and turns, you'll be making things move with levers, push-pull strips and turning circles.

In Part Three, you'll discover how to make a sliding strip move on a curved line instead of just a straight line. By adding brass fasteners to strips, you'll find new patterns of motion and action.

If you want to make a complex pop-up, try making a pop-up super structure in the middle of the paper with a sliding strip or a turning circle on the side. Then you'll have more than one action in your pop-up!

Tips

- Make cuts in the middle of the page with a cutting blade, such as an Olfa touch knife. Make sure an adult supervises. If you don't have a cutting blade, use a pair of scissors.
- Cut all lines neatly. If the cut line for the curved sliding strip is jagged, the sliding figure will catch on the paper.
- If you are following a pattern, be as exact and careful in your cutting as possible.
- When you attach the outside paper to your pop-up, be sure not to apply glue on or near the sliding strip or turning circle. The strip or circle won't move if it is stuck to the outer paper.
- Be careful where you place your circles or sliding strips on your page. Figures will not move smoothly if they are folded.
- In most cases, it is better to use a small brass fastener rather than a large one.

Make a Face with Changing Eyes

1 Take two pieces of paper, each 21.5 cm x 28 cm (8½ in. x 11 in.). Fold each paper in half. Put one aside.

2 On the folded edge, mark a dot 7.5 cm (3 in.) from the bottom of the paper.

3 From this dot, draw a 5 cm (2 in.) line towards the middle of the page. Cut the line.

4 Now follow steps 3 to 6 on page 95 to make a pop-up mouth.

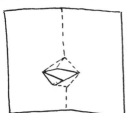

5 Take another piece of paper (a different colour from the pop-up mouth) that is 21.5 cm x 28 cm (8½ in. x 11 in.). On this paper, draw a circle with a diameter of 14.5 cm (5¾ in.) (use a compass or trace around a large can or lid). Cut out the circle.

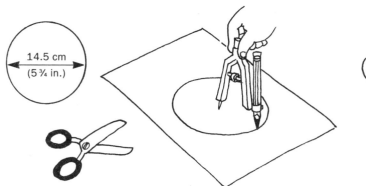

6 Mark the middle of the circle with a dot. Place the circle behind the pop-up mouth. The edge of the circle should be just above the edge of your page and the dot should be on the fold.

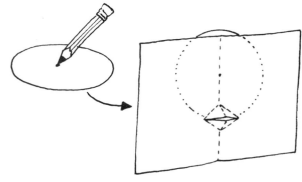

7 Hold the paper with the circle behind it up to a light or against a window. You should be able to see the dot in the middle of the circle. Mark it with a dot on your paper, then put the circle aside.

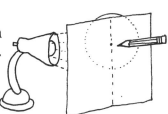

8 Draw two eyes on either side of the dot. The eyes can be circles or ovals. Cut out the eyes using either a cutting blade or pointed scissors.

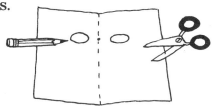

9 Poke a small hole in the middle of the circle. Poke another small hole through the dot between the eyes. Put a small brass paper fastener first through the hole in the paper, then through the hole in the circle. Open the arms of the fastener and place them so that they lie just off the fold line.

back view

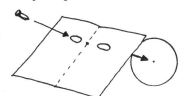

10 Draw a pair of eyeballs on the part of the circle that shows through the cut eyes. Turn the circle and draw another pair of eyeballs. Continue doing this until you have at least four pairs of eyeballs. Try using different colours and ideas for eyeballs.

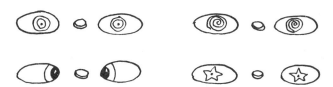
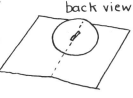

11 Draw and colour the rest of the face. You can make glasses around the eyes and the brass fastener. Draw lines around the edge of your circle to create teeth, if you like.

12 Turn the paper over. Apply glue around the edge of the paper, *being careful to keep it away from the circle area*. Carefully put the paper you have put aside on top of the glued paper. Press firmly. When you turn the circle, you will see changing eyeballs. When you close the paper, you will have a small lump in the middle because of the brass fastener.

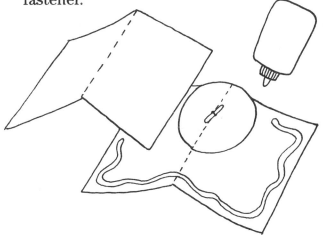

13 Decorate the inside and outside papers.

Make a Curved Sliding Strip

1 Take two pieces of paper, each 21.5 cm x 28 cm (8½ in. x 11 in.). Fold each paper in half. Put one aside.

2 Take another piece of heavy paper, 10 cm x 10 cm (4 in. x 4 in.). On this paper, draw a circle with a diameter of 6 to 8 cm (2¼ in. to 3⅛ in.) (use a compass or trace around a can or lid). Cut out the circle. Mark the middle of the circle with a dot.

3 Place the circle under the bottom right edge of your paper. The edge of your circle should be just below the bottom of your paper.

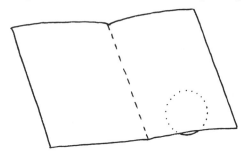

4 Hold the paper with the circle behind it up to a light or against a window. You should be able to see the dot in the middle of your circle. Mark it with a dot on your paper.

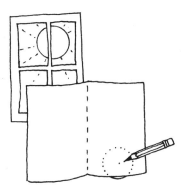

5 Poke a small hole in the middle of the circle. Poke another small hole through the dot on your page. Put a small brass paper fastener first through the hole in the paper, then through the hole in the circle. Open the arms of the fastener.

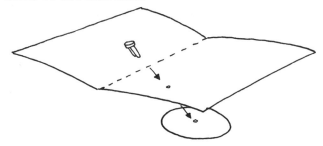

6 Cut a strip of Bristol board 2 cm x 6 cm (¾ in. x 2¼ in.). Apply tape to the end of the strip and place it on the back of the circle as shown. Reinforce the strip with a piece of tape.

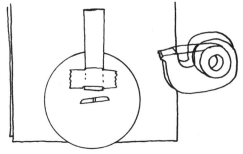

7 From the edge of the circle, measure up the strip 2 cm (¾ in.) and mark a dot on the edge of the strip. Make a very small cut in the strip at the dot.

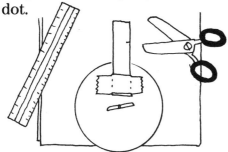

8 Place the strip on the left of the page as shown. Put the tip of a pencil into the small cut on the strip. Draw a curved line by holding the pencil and strip with both hands and pulling them to the right. *Do not go as far as the bottom of the page.*

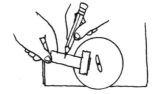

9 Turn the strip to the bottom of the page. Cut the curved line with a cutting knife or sharp scissors. Do not cut through the strip.

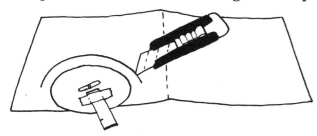

10 Insert the strip through the curved line and turn the paper over. Turn the edge of the circle and the strip will swing in a curve.

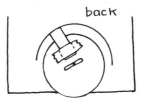
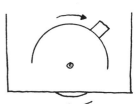

11 Take a heavy piece of paper, 7.5 cm x 5 cm (3 in. x 2 in.). On the paper, draw, colour and cut out a small person, animal or object. Apply glue to the top of the strip and place the figure on it. Allow the glue to dry before turning the circle.

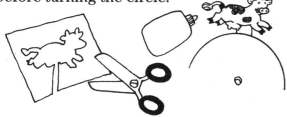

12 In the area of the brass fastener, draw a picture. You could create such scenes as a cow jumping over the moon, a ball going over a fence, a spaceship flying over a planet or a car going over a ramp.

13 Carefully apply glue around the edges of the back of your paper, being careful to keep it away from the circle and turning strip. *Make sure that you do not apply glue in the area of the turning strip.* Glue your paper to the paper you put aside. Press firmly.

14 Decorate the inside and outside papers.

Make a Juggler

1 Take two pieces of paper, each 21.5 cm x 28 cm (8½ in. x 11 in.). Fold each paper in half. Put one aside.

2 Open the other paper and on the right side of it, about 7 cm (2¾ in.) down from the top, draw a horizontal line 10 cm (4 in.) long. Cut the line with a cutting knife or sharp scissors.

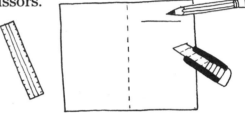

3 Take a heavy piece of paper, 10 cm x 10 cm (4 in. x 4 in.). On this paper, draw a circle with a diameter of 6 to 8 cm (2¼ to 3⅛ in.) (use a compass or trace around a large can or lid). Cut out the circle. Mark the middle of the circle with a dot.

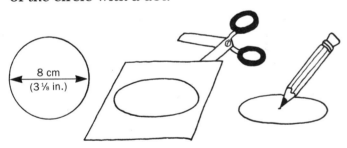

8 cm (3⅛ in.)

4 Draw a dot 1 cm (⅜ in.) from the edge of the circle. With a cutting blade or pointed scissors, poke a small hole at the dot. Poke a hole at the dot in the middle of the circle as well.

5 To make a sliding strip to turn your circle, cut a piece of Bristol board or cardboard, 14 cm x 2 cm (5½ in. x ¾ in.).

6 Draw a dot 1 cm (⅜ in.) away from the edge of the strip. Poke a small hole at the dot.

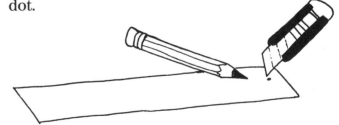

7 Put a small brass paper fastener first through the hole in the strip, then through the hole close to the edge of the circle. Open the arms of the fastener.

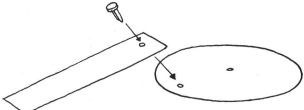

8 From behind the paper, slip the top of the circle through the slot you cut in step 2. The strip should be behind the paper on the right side of the circle.

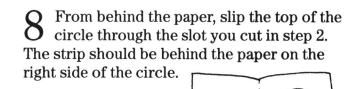

9 Hold the paper with the circle behind it up to a light or against a window. You should be able to see the dot in the middle of the circle. Mark it with a dot on your paper, then put the circle aside.

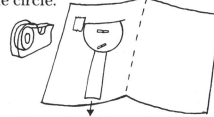

10 Poke a small hole at this dot. Put another small brass paper fastener first through the hole in the paper and then through the middle hole in the circle. Open the arms of the fastener.

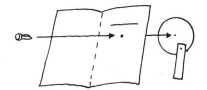

11 Turn the paper over. Pull the strip down and place a piece of tape over the slot to the left of the circle (to stop the strip from moving too high). Do not put tape on the circle.

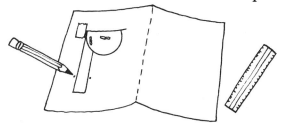

12 Push the strip up as far as the slot on the left side of the circle. From the bottom of the strip, measure up 4 cm (1 ½ in.) and mark dots on both sides of the strip.

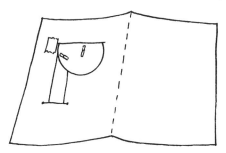

13 Move the strip to the side and draw a line between the two dots. Cut the line with a cutting blade or sharp scissors.

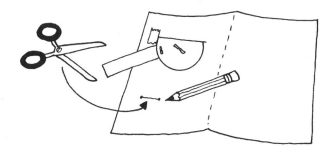

14 Insert the end of the strip through the slot to the other side of the paper.

15 Turn the paper over. Draw a double-headed arrow at the bottom of the strip, as shown.

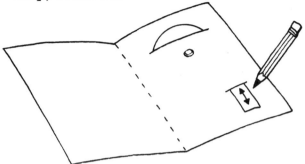

16 Push the strip up and draw coloured balls along the top of the circle. Pull the strip down and draw more coloured balls on the rest of the circle.

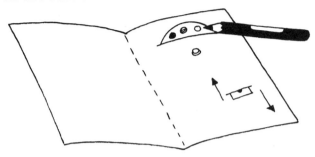

17 Below the circle, draw a person with his hands up in a juggling position. You can draw some balls on the paper as well.

18 Apply glue to the back of your paper. Glue it to the paper you put aside, which now becomes the outside paper. *Do not apply glue in the area of the strip and circle.*

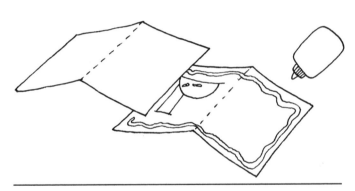

19 Decorate the inside and outside papers.

Other Ideas

Draw fireworks on the turning circle.

More Super Pop-ups
Using Sliding Strips

Two Attached Strips

One strip can be attached to another strip with a brass fastener for double action on the page. The bottom strip will swing back and forth.

Make a Pocket

Make a paper pocket on the page. Then a figure on a strip can slide into the pocket and disappear.

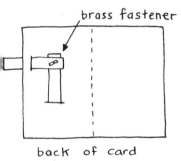

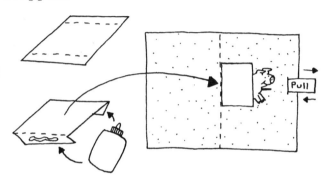

Make a Swinging Thing

You can make an object on a page swing back and forth by using a brass fastener, tape and a strip of Bristol board. Insert the brass fastener through the object, then through the base paper and finally through one end of the strip. Spread the arms of the fastener and tape them to the strip, as shown in the close-up. You can make a tail wagging on a dog or a tree falling down.

Make a Victorian Turning Circle

1 Take a heavy piece of paper or Bristol board 30 cm x 20 cm (12 in. x 8 in.) and fold it in half. This will be your base paper.

2 Take two pieces of heavy white paper 21.5 cm x 28 cm (8½ in. x 11 in.). Photocopy or carefully trace and cut out the pattern pieces on pages 71 and 72 for the turning circle. Mark the pieces A, B, C and D with an erasable pencil.

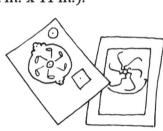

3 Cut the lines inside circle A and in pattern B using a cutting blade. It is easier to do the cutting if you lightly tape the pattern pieces to a piece of Bristol board. Make sure that your cutting is very exact.

Bristol board

4 Cut out pieces C and D using scissors.

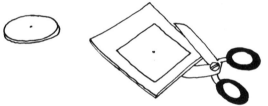

5 Remember to mark the middle of pieces C and D with a dot as in the pattern. Poke a hole at each dot using a sharp object or a cutting knife.

6 Using an erasable pencil, mark pieces A and B with the numbers 1 to 6 as shown.

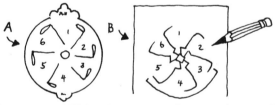

A   B

7 Place piece A on piece B so that the pull tabs are at the top and bottom of the page.

8 Now you will be inserting the sections of piece B up through the sections of piece A. Carefully pull section 1 from piece B up and through the left side of section 1 from piece A as shown.

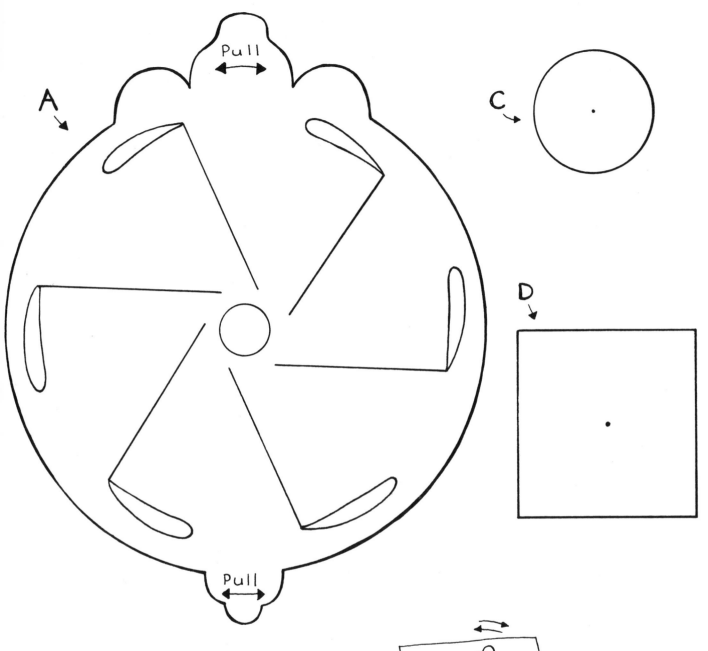

A

Pull

C

D

Pull

Pull

9 Insert section 2 of piece B through the left side of section 2 of piece A. Continue going around the circle in the same way from section 3 to section 6 until all of the sections are inserted.

If the sections have been inserted properly, you should be able to hold the pull tabs and move the top circle back and forth freely.

B

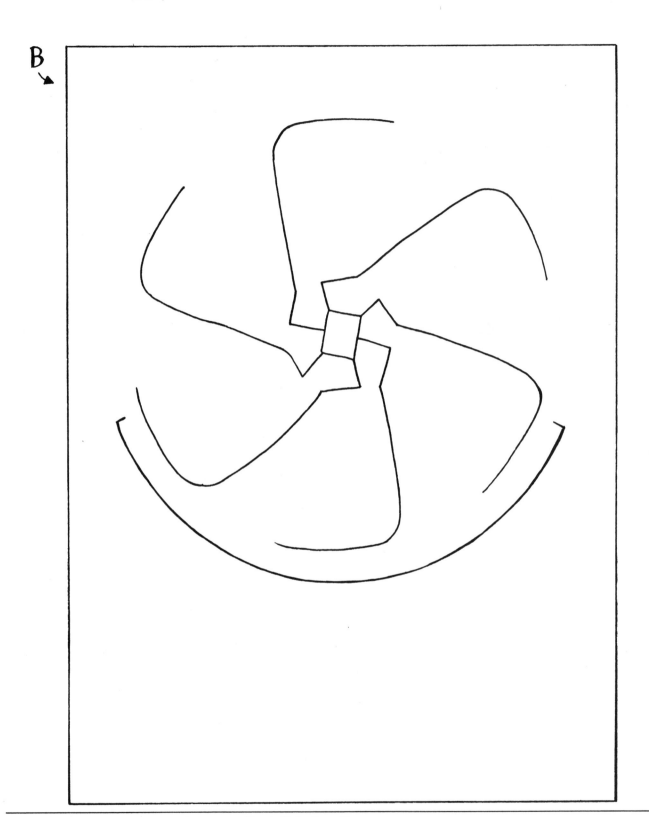

10 Take a small brass fastener and insert it through the hole in piece C. Place piece D under the middle of piece B. Insert the brass fastener through the middle of pieces A, B and D and open the arms. The circle pieces should be able to move back and forth. You may have to jiggle or move them a little to make them slide.

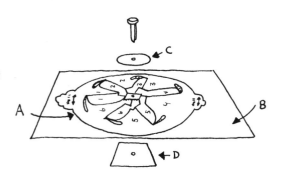

11 Carefully erase the numbers on pieces A and B.

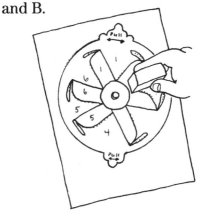

12 Pull the tabs and turn the circle until only piece A sections are showing. Draw a design or picture on the sections.

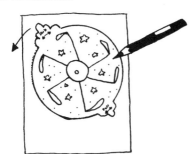

13 Pull the tabs and turn them in the opposite direction until only the sections from piece B are showing. Draw a completely different design or picture on these sections.

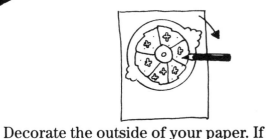

14 Open the base paper. Apply glue around the edge of the back of the turning circle paper. *Make sure that you do not apply glue near the turning sections.* Now place the turning circle paper on the right side of the open base paper. Press firmly. When you hold the pull tabs and turn the circles, you should see two changing patterns. You may want to decorate the circle piece in the middle of the changing patterns (piece C).

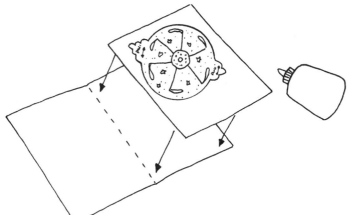

15 Decorate the outside of your paper. If your circle sections stick, try jiggling the paper. Check to make sure that the sections have been inserted properly.

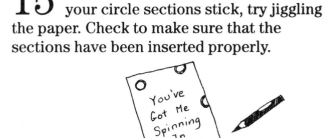

Other Ideas

You can put the turning circle on the outside of your base paper instead of inside.

73

Part Four Superbly Different Pop-ups

Did you know that you can make noisy pop-ups or pop-ups that snap on rubber bands? You can also make super pop-ups out of many household objects that you would normally throw away. Save your Popsicle sticks, envelopes and small boxes for pop-up projects.

Super pop-ups can also be used in drama productions. In Part Four, you'll find ideas for masks and props. You'll also discover how to use large pop-ups in posters, bulletin boards or table displays. Think big!

Pop-ups don't have to be used only for pop-up cards and books. You can also use them for posters, displays, masks, drama props, games and much, much more. Read on to find out how.

Tips

- If you are making big super pop-ups, you must use heavy Bristol board or cardboard. Use materials such as white glue, masking tape and twist-ties to join pop-up parts together.
- If you don't have large pieces of Bristol board available for making really big pop-ups, join pieces of Bristol board together using staples.
- For large pop-ups, you may want to staple pieces together and then reinforce them with masking tape.
- When using recycled objects for pop-ups, cover any advertising or print with paper, decorations or paint.
- Save interesting objects to add to your pop-up masks! Try using feathers, sequins, lace, buttons and ribbon.
- When cutting large pop-ups, use a heavy cutting knife or large scissors. Make sure an adult helps you.
- With drama productions, try writing scenes that will use pop-up ideas.

Make a Noisy Robot

1 Fold a piece of Bristol board 40 cm x 30 cm (16 in. x 12 in.) in half. Set it aside.

2 To make arms for your robot, use two pieces of Bristol board, 2.5 cm x 13 cm (1 in. x 5⅛ in.). Along one side of each strip, cut small notches to create a jagged edge. Make sure that you make many small notches and not a few large notches.

3 Take two Popsicle sticks. Apply glue to one side of each stick and place on the end of the Bristol board strips as shown. Reinforce the ends of the sticks with tape.

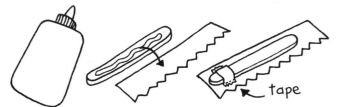

tape

4 Fold the ends of the strips up to create tabs.

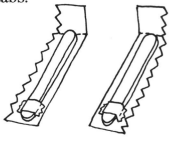

5 Open the Bristol board. Place the arms in the middle of the Bristol board with the jagged edges pointing towards the top of the page and the tabs along the fold line. Apply glue to the back of the tabs and place them on the base paper as shown. Reinforce the tabs with pieces of tape.

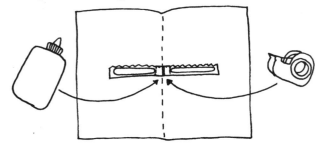

6 To make your robot's body, fold in half a heavy piece of paper or light Bristol board, 21.5 cm x 11.5 cm (8½ in. x 4½ in.).

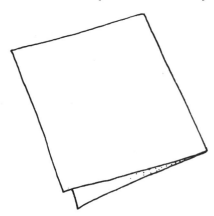

7 Draw a line 2 cm (¾ in.) from each end of the paper. Fold back along these lines to create tabs.

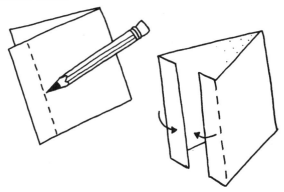

8 Now you will make openings in the body for the arms. From the top of the middle fold on the body, measure down 4 cm (1½ in.) and mark a dot.

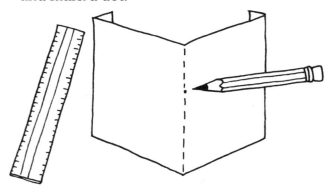

9 From this dot, measure across 3.5 cm (1 ¼ in.) on each side, marking dots.

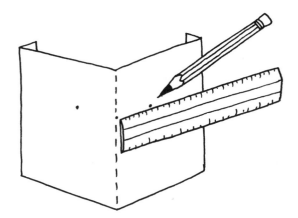

10 Down from each of these dots, draw lines that are 2.5 cm (1 in.) long.

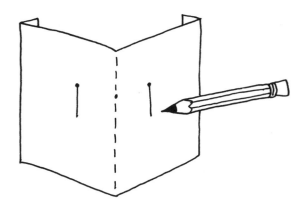

11 Above each line, draw the following shape with the measurements shown. Cut all of the lines using a cutting blade.

1 cm (⅜ in.)

1.6 cm (⅝ in.)

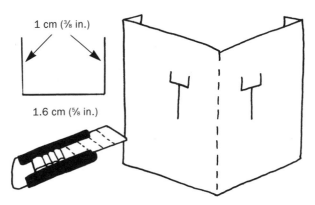

12 Decorate the body, drawing buttons and dials.

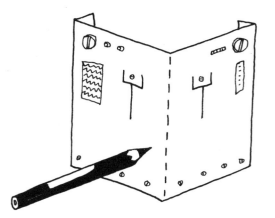

13 On the base paper, mark a dot 6.5 cm (2½ in.) to the left of the middle fold line, in the middle of the paper. Mark another dot 6.5 cm (2½ in.) to the right of the middle.

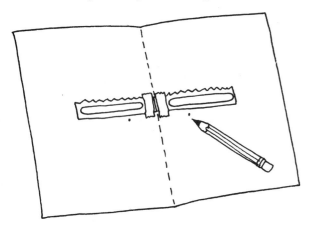

14 Carefully insert the arms through the cut sections of the body. Apply glue to the bottom tabs of the body and place the tabs at the dots. Reinforce the tabs with tape. The arms should slide through the cut section with the jagged edge hitting the small flaps of paper. The motion of the jagged arms hitting the small flaps of paper on the body will create a noise.

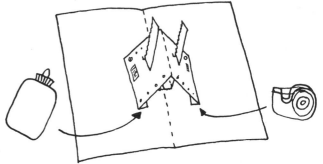

15 Make a head for the robot that is about 5 cm x 7.5 cm (2 in. x 3 in.) and legs that are about 9 cm x 6 cm (3½ in. x 2¼ in.). Fold the head in half. Decorate the head and legs and glue them to the body, being careful to match the fold on the head to the fold of the body. You can also make small hands to add to the ends of the arms.

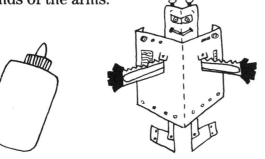

16 Decorate the inside and outside of the Bristol board. You can put pieces of tape between the body and the Bristol board for extra reinforcement. If your robot does not make noise, try placing the body on the Bristol board again in a different position. The arms must catch on the flaps of paper but they must also move in and out.

Other Ideas

Add Pop-up Eyes

Make a face with eyeballs that click and pop out. Add a nose, mouth and hair.

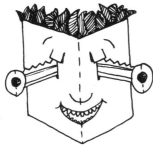

Add a Sign

You can make a sign on a string. Attach the ends of the string to the hands with tape.

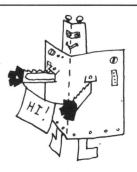

Make a Snapping Sports Car

1 Take two pieces of Bristol board, 40 cm x 30 cm (16 in. x 12 in.) and fold them in half. Put one aside.

2 Open the other piece of Bristol board. Draw a diagonal line 21.5 cm (8½ in.) long on the right side of the paper, as shown. Draw another line the same length parallel to the first one. The two lines should be about .3 cm (⅛ in.) apart from one another. Using a ruler and a cutting blade, cut the two lines. Cut across the ends of both lines and remove the strip of paper.

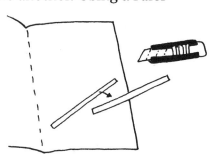

3 From a rubber or elastic band about .3 cm (⅛ in.) wide, cut a piece 7 cm (2¾ in.) long.

4 Fold in half a piece of Bristol board, 7.5 cm x 2 cm (3 in. x ¾ in.). Staple one end of the band to one end of the Bristol board as shown. Use several staples and reinforce the staples with tape.

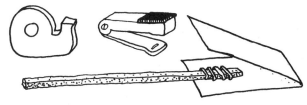

5 Fold the piece of Bristol board closed and staple it shut.

6 Turn over the Bristol board with the diagonal cut. Place the Bristol board with the band at the top end of the cut as shown and staple it in place.

back view

7 To make the car, fold in half a piece of heavy paper, 11 cm x 6.5 cm (4¼ in. x 2½ in.). Draw and cut out the following car shape.

8 Fold up the bottom 2 cm (¾ in.) of the car on both sides to create tabs. Colour and decorate both sides of the car so that it will look like a sports car. Apply glue to the inside of the car and press it closed. Do not apply glue to the tab area.

9 Fold in half a second piece of Bristol board, 7.5 cm x 2 cm (3 in. x ¾ in.). Staple the free end of the rubber band to one end of the piece of Bristol board so that the strip of rubber band between the two pieces of Bristol board is 3 cm (1⅛ in.) long. Reinforce the Bristol board with tape.

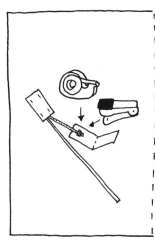

10 Fold the piece of Bristol board closed and staple it shut.

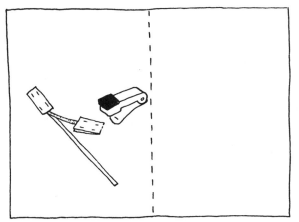

11 Place this piece of Bristol board on the bottom of the tabs of the car as shown and staple it in place. Reinforce the staples with tape.

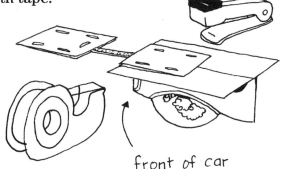

front of car

12 Insert the car shape through the slot. The tabs should stay under the paper.

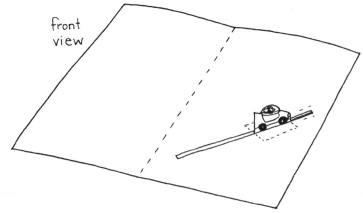

front view

13 Apply glue to the back of your paper. Glue it to the paper you put aside, which now becomes the outside paper. *Do not apply glue in the area of the strip and circle.* If necessary, staple the edges of the papers as well. You can also staple the middle area of the paper on either side of the diagonal cut. Make sure that you do not staple the tabs of the car. Because of the pull of the elastic band, it is necessary to have all pieces stapled and taped securely.

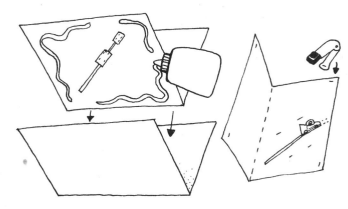

14 Print "Pull" on the back of the car. Pull the car back to the end of the slot. Let go and the car will "snap" forward. If your car does not move smoothly, your rubber band may be too long or too short.

15 Decorate the inside and outside papers. After opening your paper, stand your car in an upright position.

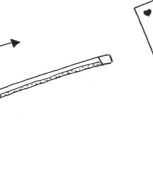

Other Ideas

Rocket Ship

Make a rocket ship fly upward.

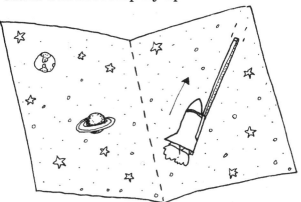

Zoom

Glue a small ZOOM! sign to the back of the moving figure.

Make a Monster from an Envelope

1 Take a heavy piece of paper 30 cm x 23 cm (12 in. x 9 in.) and fold it in half lengthwise. Put it aside.

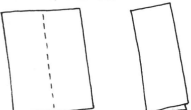

2 Take an envelope that is new or used. (Used envelopes should have been opened from the top of the envelope.) Both square and rectangular envelopes will make pop-ups. Turn to the back of the envelope.

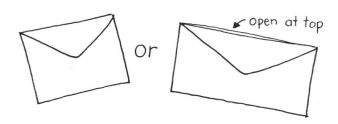

3 If the envelope is a used one, draw a line across the bottom of the closing flap as shown. If you are using a new envelope, open the flap and draw a line across the bottom of the opening as shown.

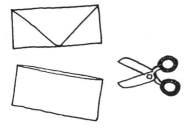

4 Starting at the edge of the envelope, cut along this line through the front and back. Put the top of the envelope aside.

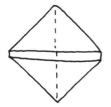
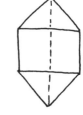

5 Open the bottom part of the envelope by holding the edges in the middle and pulling outward.

6 Carefully flatten the top and bottom, to create triangles. The middle fold of the triangles should match the middle fold of the envelope.

The shapes vary depending on the envelope.

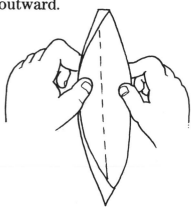

Square Envelope   Rectangular Envelope

7 Decorate the envelope. You can turn it into a monster by colouring it and adding eyes, nose and antennae. If you have writing on your envelope, cover it with paper decorations.

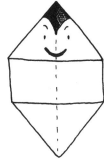

8 From the envelope piece that you put aside, cut jagged strips of teeth and glue them onto the edges of the mouth. You can also glue a tongue-shaped piece of paper inside the mouth.

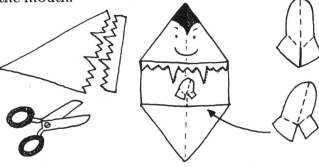

9 Open the piece of paper that you put aside. Apply glue to the back of the monster envelope. Place the envelope in the middle area of the paper, matching the fold lines. Press the envelope firmly. Close the paper and press firmly.

10 If your mouth does not pop out, insert your fingers into the top and bottom triangles and pull them towards you.

11 Decorate the inside and outside papers.

Other Ideas

You can add paper ears above the envelope to create different characters.

Make a Story Box

1 Fold in half a piece of Bristol board, 40 cm x 25 cm (16 in. x 10 in.). Set it aside.

2 Take a small box or carton such as those used for holding biscuits, cookies or Popsicles. The box must be made from paperboard, not heavy corrugated cardboard. Cut off the flaps at both ends of the box.

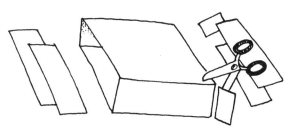

3 Draw a rectangle on one side of the box as shown. The rectangle should be as tall as the side of the box, but 1 cm (⅜ in.) narrower at each end. Using sharp scissors, cut out the rectangle.

4 Apply glue to the side of the box opposite the cut rectangle. Place that side at the bottom of the left side of the Bristol board. Press firmly. Secure the glued area with tape or staples.

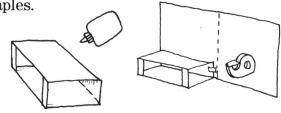

5 Now you will be creating the picture story. Think of a story that you can tell in three scenes. Push the box upward until it is lying flat against the base paper. Inside the area framed by the rectangle, draw and colour the first scene of your story. Write "1" in the corner of your picture.

6 Pull the box down to the middle position. Carefully draw and colour your second picture on the back panel and write "2" in the corner. You may have to reach in from the sides of the box to draw this picture.

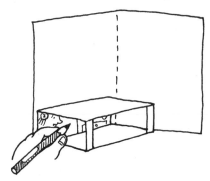

7 Pull the box down until it is lying flat. Draw and colour your third picture inside the frame. Write "3" in the corner.

8 Cover the outside of the box with paper or giftwrap. Glue or tape it in place. Make sure that you leave a neatly trimmed opening around the rectangle.

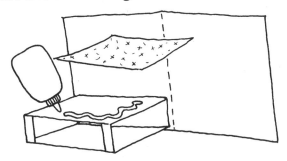

9 Take a piece of heavy paper 5 cm x 5 cm (2 in. x 2 in.) and cut out the shape shown to create a tab. Print "Pull" on the bottom of the tab. Apply glue to the back of the top of the tab and place it on the box under the first scene, as shown.

10 Write out your story to go on the right side of your page. Divide it into three sections numbered 1, 2 and 3 to go with the pictures.

11 Decorate the outside of your box picture story.

You can use almost any size box for this super pop-up. Make sure you change the size of your base paper to fit it.

Make Pop-up Masks

You can make masks with pop-up pieces glued on for interesting noses and mouths. The masks can later be folded and stored. Follow the Basic Pattern, then add pieces to create interesting masks. Be sure to cut large eye holes so you can see clearly.

Basic Pattern

1 Fold in half a heavy piece of paper, 21.5 cm x 28 cm (8½ in. x 11 in.).

2 Place the paper so that the folded edge is on your left. Draw the lines shown below, starting at the folded edge. The lines should not go past the middle of the page. Cut the lines starting from the folded edge.

3 Fold the cut strip forward and then back to its original position.

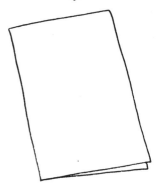

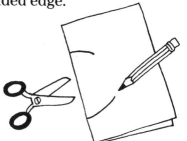

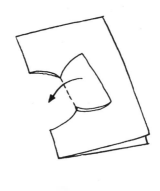

4 Open your paper and hold it like a tent. Push the strip down in the opposite direction of the fold, so that it is pushed through to the other side of the paper. Close the paper and press firmly. Open to see the pop-up shape. This is the nose of your mask.

5 Cut the edges of the paper to create different shapes, as shown. Be sure to cut out large eye holes, too. Now use this basic pattern to create any mask you like.

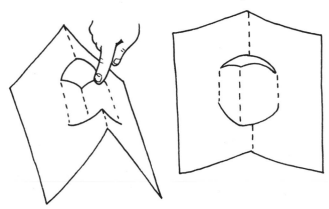

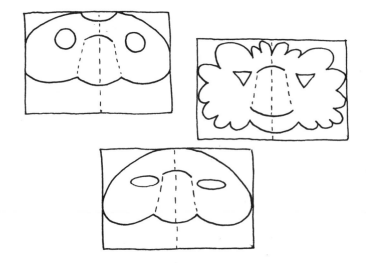

Bird Mask

1 Make the Basic Pattern (see page 86, steps 1 to 4), then cut the mask shape shown below.

2 Cut out a beak similar to the shape below. Fold the beak in half vertically. Apply glue on the top of the back of the beak. Place the beak as shown on the pop-up shape of your mask, so that the folds match.

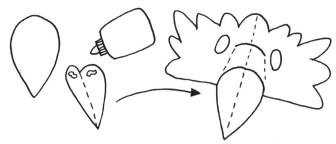

3 Add paper feathers to the top of the mask.

4 To create an extra fold in the beak, fold the tip of the beak to the right, then fold it back to its original position. Open the bottom of the beak and you will see a small triangle. Push in the long edge of the triangle to create the extra fold.

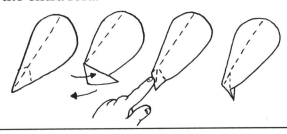

Elephant Mask

1 Make the Basic Pattern (see page 86, steps 1 to 4). Then cut the mask shape shown below.

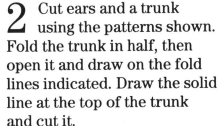

2 Cut ears and a trunk using the patterns shown. Fold the trunk in half, then open it and draw on the fold lines indicated. Draw the solid line at the top of the trunk and cut it.

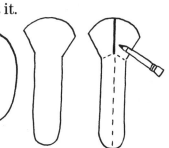

ears

3 Fold the trunk in half again and place it so that the folded edge is on the left. Fold the end of the trunk up to the right, then fold it back to its original position. Open the trunk and you will see a small triangle at the bottom. Push in the round edge of the triangle to create a fold.

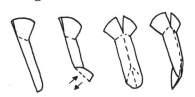

4 Apply glue to the tip as shown. Pinch the glued area together.

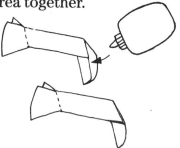

5 Glue the top flaps of the trunk to the mask, matching the fold lines.

6 Glue the ears to the mask as shown.

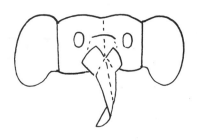

Alligator Mask

1 Make the Basic Pattern (see page 86, steps 1 to 4), then cut the mask shape shown below.

2 Draw and cut the following jaws. Draw the fold lines to create tabs.

3 Fold the rounded tabs forward, then fold them back to their original position. Fold the straight tabs forward, then fold them back to their original position. Open both jaws flat.

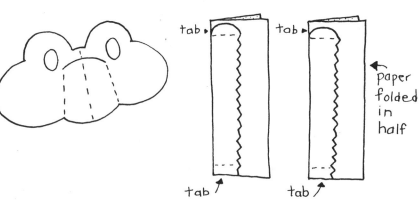

4 Apply glue to the straight tabs of one jaw. Press the glued areas together as shown. Repeat this with the other jaw.

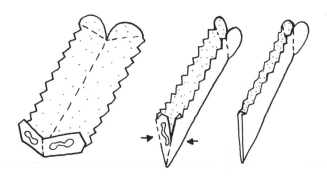

5 Apply glue to the rounded flaps of one jaw and attach it as shown so that it becomes the upper jaw. Apply glue to the rounded flaps of the other jaw. Attach the flaps as shown so that this jaw becomes the bottom one. Reinforce the glued areas with tape.

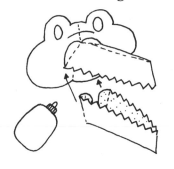

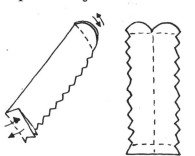

Make Enormous Pop-ups for the Stage

The great thing about pop-up props is that they can be folded and neatly stored. When you make very large pop-ups, remember to use heavy materials such as corrugated cardboard, masking tape and twist-ties.

Basic Box Structure

1 For a base, you can use a large piece of corrugated cardboard from a box such as one used for holding a refrigerator. Cut it so that the piece has a fold in the middle.

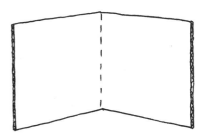

2 Cut the flaps off both ends of a medium-sized corrugated box.

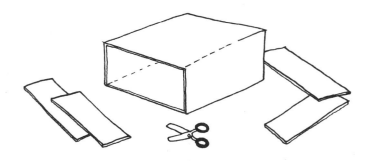

3 Push the box down until it is lying flat. Now you know which way the box folds naturally.

4 Open the box again and place one side along the fold line of the cardboard base. The box should fold when the base is folded.

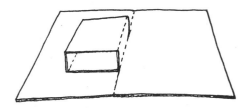

5 To attach the box to the base, make two holes in the upper inside edge of the box using a sharp object such as a compass. Have an adult help you make two holes in the base as well, immediately behind the other two holes.

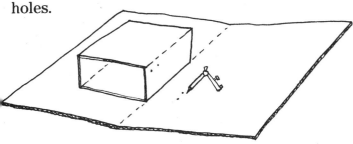

6 Push a twist-tie through the holes and twist it shut at the back of the base cardboard.

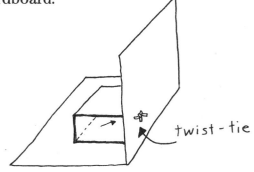

twist-tie

7 Put a twist-tie in the other upper corner as well.

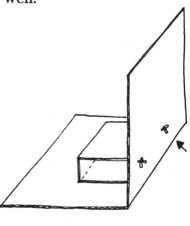

8 Put one twist-tie in the middle of the bottom of the box as shown. If you wish, secure the structure with masking tape. If you are using a very large box as a base, you can use more twist-ties to secure the structure.

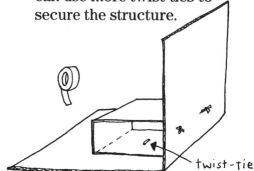

twist-tie

9 Close the base and press firmly. If the box does not fold properly, adjust the twist-ties so that they are not fastened as tightly. You now have a pop-up structure that can be used in a number of ways.

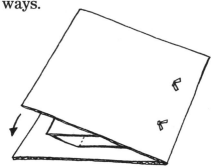

Make a Tree Grow

In a play, you could create a scene in which a character opens a flap on the floor to suddenly reveal a tree.

1 Make a box structure as described on pages 89 to 90.

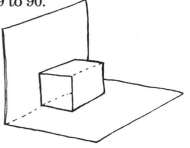

2 Draw, colour and cut out a giant tree on a rigid piece of cardboard. The size of the tree is limited by the size of the box that you use in your box structure.

3 Apply white glue to the back of the tree at the bottom and place it against the front of the box structure. Secure the tree with masking tape as well.

4 Place your base along a wall so that when you open the pop-up, you can secure it to the wall with masking tape or hooks and your tree will remain upright.

Make a Quick Hiding Place

Use a box for a pop-up structure that is large enough to hold a person lying down. Make a box structure following the instructions on pages 89 to 90. If a character in your play suddenly needs a hiding place, she can open the base cardboard and hook the back to the wall. Then the character can climb inside the box and hide.

Furniture and Appliances

Tables, chairs, stoves, etc., can be made with box structures. Hook the base of the box structure to the wall during the play.

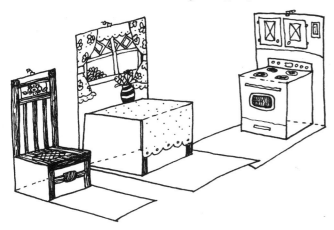

Fold-out Forest

Create a fold-out forest using a number of box structures.

Store Fronts

Make a town scene with store fronts using a number of box structures.

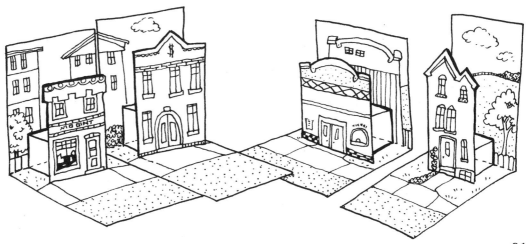

More Super Pop-ups in Drama

Windows

If a character in your play is lost, a pop-up can help her find her way. When she opens a window, out springs a pop-up strip (see page 94) with an arrow attached to one side and the name of a place.

Hats

Does a detective in your play need a hiding place for a key or other object? Make a hat as shown then cut a flap on the top. Turn the hat upside down and glue a piece of paper to the inside, over the flap you cut. Turn the hat over again and open the flap. Make a paper spring (see page 94) and glue it to the paper under the flap. Tape the object onto the paper spring. Close the flap and secure it with a piece of tape. When you open the flap, the object will spring up.

Costumes

If one character is madly in love with another character, he can open a card on his chest to show a pop-up heart!

the tube should be large enough to fit around your head

Giant Pop-ups for Displays

Make a Giant Dragon

Are you studying dragons at school? Using a large piece of Bristol board or a large piece of heavy paper, make a giant dragon head by following the instructions on pages 19 to 21 but increasing the measurements. Use more of the same kind of paper to make a large body. It's fun to cut out shiny scales from foil or metallic paper to cover the body of the dragon.

Make a Giant Pop-up Mouth

Take a large, heavy piece of paper or Bristol board and make a giant pop-up mouth by following the instructions on page 95 but increasing the measurements. Draw a face around the mouth and colour it.

You can use your giant pop-up mouth as part of a poster or display. You can also use it as a game. How many buttons or coins can you and your friends toss into it? Move back if it's too easy!

Or use your giant pop-up mouth for a suggestion box. Draw a large face around the mouth and have people drop in their ideas.

Make Pop-up Posters

Make a giant "Read a Good Book" pop-up to advertise a reading program, a library event or a book club. See page 22 for instructions.

Make a Super School Project

For a table display, you can create a super pop-up model. If your project is about your town, for instance, build a model of one of the streets. To do this, make wide pop-up strips (see page 94) for the buildings. Glue the pop-ups into a low box to form the base. Add toy cars, pop-ups on sliding strips (see page 96) and people to your display.

You can also use super pop-ups to make a bulletin-board display. Attach your pop-ups to the bulletin board and surround them with information about your project.

BASIC POP-UP TECHNIQUES

Here are four pop-up techniques that you'll find very useful.

Pop-up Strip

1 Fold in half a piece of paper, 21.5 cm x 28 cm (8½ x 11 in.). In the middle of the *folded edge*, mark two dots .6 cm (¼ in.) apart.

2 Starting at the dots, draw two lines, each 2.5 cm (1 in.) long, towards the edge of the paper. Cut the lines starting from the folded edge.

3 Fold the cut strip back and then fold it forward again.

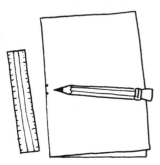

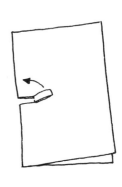

4 Open your paper and hold it like a tent. Push the strip through to the other side of your paper. Close the paper and press firmly. Open to see the pop-up strip.

5 Draw, colour and cut out a figure or object. The figure can be a little taller and wider than your strip. Apply glue on one side of the strip. Place the figure on the glue.

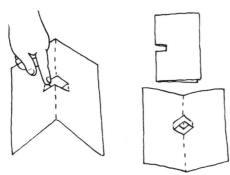

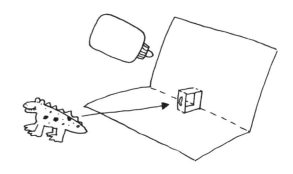

Pop-up Spring

Cut two strips of paper, each 7 cm x 1 cm (2¾ x ⅜ in.). Apply glue at the end of one strip, then lay the other on top at right angles. Fold the strips as shown.

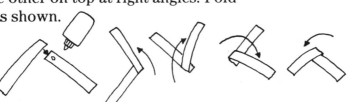

Pop-up Mouth

1 Fold in half a piece of paper, 21.5 cm x 28 cm (8½ x 11 in.). Put a dot in approximately the centre of the folded edge.

2 Draw a 5 cm (2 in.) line from the dot towards the outer edge. Starting at the folded edge, cut on the line.

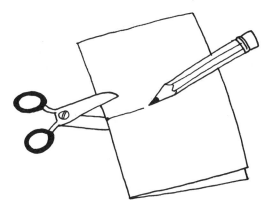

3 Fold back the flaps to form two triangles.

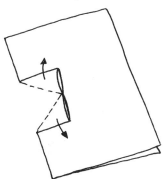

4 Fold the flaps back to their original position. Open the whole paper.

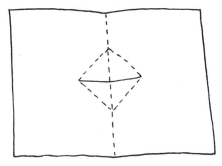

5 Hold your paper, so that it looks like a tent. Put your finger on the top triangle and push down. Pinch the two folded edges of the top triangle, so that the triangle is pushed through to the other side of the paper.

6 Put your finger on the bottom triangle and do the same thing. The top and bottom triangles will now be pushed out to form a mouth inside the paper. When you open and close your paper, the mouth will look like it is talking.

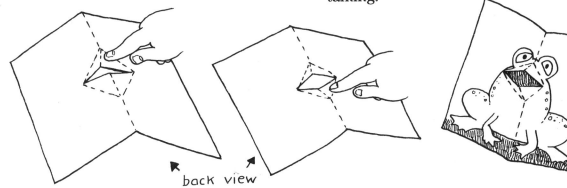

back view

95

Sliding Strip

1 Take a piece of paper, 21.5 cm x 28 cm (8½ x 11 in.). Fold in half then open it again.

2 Draw a long line, about 10 cm (4 in.), diagonally across the right side of your paper. Cut this line with a cutting blade or with a pointed pair of scissors. This is your large slot. Cut a small vertical slot, 3 cm (1⅛ in.) long, near the end of the large slot.

3 Draw a figure or object on a heavy piece of paper, 5 cm x 5 cm (2 in. x 2 in.). The figure should be about 4 cm (1½ in.) long. Colour it and cut it out.

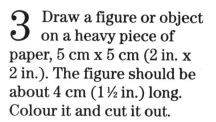

4 Now make a sliding strip that will help your figure move across the page. To make the strip, cut a piece of Bristol board or cardboard, 14 cm x 2 cm (5½ in. x ¾ in.).

5 From a small piece of heavy paper, cut a tab, 4 cm x .6 cm (1½ x ¼ in.). Glue the bottom half of the tab to the left side of your strip. Fold the rest of the tab down on itself.

6 Slip the strip through the small slot. Pull the loose part of the tab through the large slot. Fold the end of the tab upward on the tab's fold line. Make sure the fold line of your tab is on the large slot.

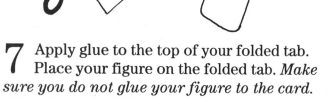

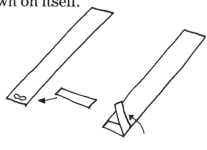

7 Apply glue to the top of your folded tab. Place your figure on the folded tab. *Make sure you do not glue your figure to the card.* Allow the glue to dry before you pull the strip.

8 Cut the end of the strip to make it shorter if necessary. Your figure should now move easily up and down the large slot of your paper.

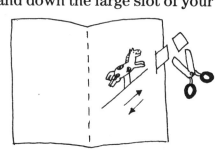